DATE DUE

| Urban Agriculture

Other Books of Related Interest:

Opposing Viewpoints Series

Nutrition

Introducing Issues with Opposing Viewpoints Series

Food Safety

At Issue Series

Can Diets Be Harmful?
Food Safety
How Can the Poor Be Helped?
Is Organic Food Better?

"Congress shall make no law … abridging the freedom of speech, or of the press."

First Amendment to the US Constitution

The basic foundation of our democracy is the First Amendment guarantee of freedom of expression. The Opposing Viewpoints Series is dedicated to the concept of this basic freedom and the idea that it is more important to practice it than to enshrine it.

Urban Agriculture

Nancy Dziedzic and Lynn M. Zott, Book Editors

GREENHAVEN PRESS
A part of Gale, Cengage Learning

GALE
CENGAGE Learning

Detroit • New York • San Francisco • New Haven, Conn • Waterville, Maine • London

Elizabeth Des Chenes, *Managing Editor*

© 2012 Greenhaven Press, a part of Gale, Cengage Learning

Gale and Greenhaven Press are registered trademarks used herein under license.

For more information, contact:
Greenhaven Press
27500 Drake Rd.
Farmington Hills, MI 48331-3535
Or you can visit our Internet site at gale.cengage.com.

For product information and technology assistance, contact us at:

Gale Customer Support, 1-800-877-4253.
For permission to use material from this text or product, submit all requests online at www.cengage.com/permissions.

Further permissions questions can be emailed to permissionrequest@cengage.com.

Articles in Greenhaven Press anthologies are often edited for length to meet page requirements. In addition, original titles of these works are changed to clearly present the main thesis and to explicitly indicate the author's opinion. Every effort is made to ensure the Greenhaven Press accurately reflects the original intent of the authors. Every effort has been made to trace the owners of copyrighted material.

Cover Image © Shannon Fagan/Corbis.

LIBRARY OF CONGRESS CATALOGING-IN-PUBLICATION DATA

Urban agriculture / Nancy Dziedzic and Lynn M. Zott, book editors.
    p. cm. -- (Opposing viewpoints)
    Includes bibliographical references and index.
    ISBN 978-0-7377-5446-9 (hardcover) -- ISBN 978-0-7377-5447-6 (pbk.)
  1. Urban agriculture. I. Dziedzic, Nancy. II. Zott, Lynn M. (Lynn Marie), 1969-
III. Series: Opposing viewpoints series (Unnumbered)
    S494.5.U72U72 2012
    635.977--dc23
                                     2011039186

Printed in the United States of America
1 2 3 4 5 6 7 16 15 14 13 12

Contents

Chapter 3: How Does Urban Agriculture Affect Particular Groups?

Why Consider Opposing Viewpoints?

> "The only way in which a human being can make some approach to knowing the whole of a subject is by hearing what can be said about it by persons of every variety of opinion and studying all modes in which it can be looked at by every character of mind. No wise man ever acquired his wisdom in any mode but this."
>
> John Stuart Mill

In our media-intensive culture it is not difficult to find differing opinions. Thousands of newspapers and magazines and dozens of radio and television talk shows resound with differing points of view. The difficulty lies in deciding which opinion to agree with and which "experts" seem the most credible. The more inundated we become with differing opinions and claims, the more essential it is to hone critical reading and thinking skills to evaluate these ideas. Opposing Viewpoints books address this problem directly by presenting stimulating debates that can be used to enhance and teach these skills. The varied opinions contained in each book examine many different aspects of a single issue. While examining these conveniently edited opposing views, readers can develop critical thinking skills such as the ability to compare and contrast authors' credibility, facts, argumentation styles, use of persuasive techniques, and other stylistic tools. In short, the Opposing Viewpoints Series is an ideal way to attain the higher-level thinking and reading skills so essential in a culture of diverse and contradictory opinions.

In addition to providing a tool for critical thinking, Opposing Viewpoints books challenge readers to question their own strongly held opinions and assumptions. Most people form their opinions on the basis of upbringing, peer pressure, and personal, cultural, or professional bias. By reading carefully balanced opposing views, readers must directly confront new ideas as well as the opinions of those with whom they disagree. This is not to argue simplistically that everyone who reads opposing views will—or should—change his or her opinion. Instead, the series enhances readers' understanding of their own views by encouraging confrontation with opposing ideas. Careful examination of others' views can lead to the readers' understanding of the logical inconsistencies in their own opinions, perspective on why they hold an opinion, and the consideration of the possibility that their opinion requires further evaluation.

Evaluating Other Opinions

To ensure that this type of examination occurs, Opposing Viewpoints books present all types of opinions. Prominent spokespeople on different sides of each issue as well as well-known professionals from many disciplines challenge the reader. An additional goal of the series is to provide a forum for other, less known, or even unpopular viewpoints. The opinion of an ordinary person who has had to make the decision to cut off life support from a terminally ill relative, for example, may be just as valuable and provide just as much insight as a medical ethicist's professional opinion. The editors have two additional purposes in including these less known views. One, the editors encourage readers to respect others' opinions—even when not enhanced by professional credibility. It is only by reading or listening to and objectively evaluating others' ideas that one can determine whether they are worthy of consideration. Two, the inclusion of such viewpoints encourages the important critical thinking skill of objectively evaluating an author's credentials and bias. This evaluation will illuminate an author's reasons for taking a particular stance on an issue and will aid in readers' evaluation of the author's ideas.

It is our hope that these books will give readers a deeper understanding of the issues debated and an appreciation of the complexity of even seemingly simple issues when good and honest people disagree. This awareness is particularly important in a democratic society such as ours in which people enter into public debate to determine the common good. Those with whom one disagrees should not be regarded as enemies but rather as people whose views deserve careful examination and may shed light on one's own.

Thomas Jefferson once said that "difference of opinion leads to inquiry, and inquiry to truth." Jefferson, a broadly educated man, argued that "if a nation expects to be ignorant and free . . . it expects what never was and never will be." As individuals and as a nation, it is imperative that we consider the opinions of others and examine them with skill and discernment. The Opposing Viewpoints Series is intended to help readers achieve this goal.

David L. Bender and Bruno Leone,
Founders

Introduction

"Urban farms have become sort of cliché
in Detroit, cast as a gardener's pipe
dream that will save the city, one batch
of arugula at a time. . . . Cliché or not,
this is a city that needs cheap, nutrient-
dense food—the kind that comes out
of the sun and soil of a farm, urban or
otherwise."

—Paul Brady, travel blogger

Detroit, Michigan, is nearly eight thousand miles away from the small Himalayan country of Nepal. Yet the two places have several things in common: high levels of poverty, a history of racial or ethnic conflict, and a thriving industry of urban agriculture. The same might be said of Cleveland and Malawi or Philadelphia and Nicaragua. The practice of urban agriculture— also called urban farming, community farming, and community gardening—has been a part of human history since the inception of urbanization thousands of years ago. Early city-dwellers recognized that importing food for a growing and densely packed population was impractical and possibly even dangerous in the case of natural disasters or war. Keeping residents' main food sources close by was essential to creating a safe, self-sustaining city.

Fast-forward to the twentieth century, and rapid industrialization ate up city land, leaving urban people to depend upon food grown in rural regions, often thousands of miles away. According to a report from the Leopold Center for Sustainable Agriculture at Iowa State University, nonlocally grown—"industrially grown"— produce generally travels about 1,494 miles to reach consumers, compared with locally grown produce, which travels about 56 miles. But what happens to a city when industry collapses and quality food becomes inaccessible? In Detroit, for example, a toxic combination of industrial failure, racial segregation, and lack of well-paying jobs left behind a diminished population of less than a million residents (from a high of 1.85 million in 1950, according to US Census figures) and at least 40 of the city's 139 square miles vacant, with approximately 17 percent of city addresses empty. Add to the mix a 2010 Census–derived poverty rate of 36.4 percent and "food desert" status with no major grocery store chains within city limits, and a fair amount of hunger and food insecurity seem inevitable.

Gregory Acs of the Urban Institute writes in "Poverty in the United States, 2008" that approximately 40 million Americans, including 14 million children, lived in poverty in that year, and urban poverty rose from 16.5 to 17.7 percent following the economic collapse of 2008. The Food and Agriculture Organization of the United Nations (FAO) blames a spike in world food prices for an international rise in hunger that began in 2007–2008. And because the economic downturn of 2008 was a global event, the urban poor around the world, who often must spend a disproportionate amount of their incomes on food due to the cost of imports, dipped even further into poverty when city jobs became scarce.

The response to the economic crisis in cities around the world, including urban centers in the United States, has been to increase the number of urban gardens—a plan that has sometimes been met with skepticism or even mockery in some American cities. In Detroit, the nationally esteemed Catherine Ferguson Academy, a public high school for pregnant and parenting girls with a full working farm on its grounds, was nearly closed down by the school district's state-appointed emergency financial manager Robert Bobb and his successor, Roy Roberts, until, at the last minute, a private company stepped in to run it as a charter school. And on a visit to the city in 2010, the Reverend

Jesse Jackson alienated those in the urban farming movement by calling the notion of agriculture in Detroit "cute but foolish," adding in a subsequent interview, "Detroit needs investment in industry, housing, and construction—not bean patches." Asenath Andrews, the principal of the Catherine Ferguson Academy since its opening in 1986, defended the concept of urban farming in a 2008 interview in *O, the Oprah Magazine,* saying that she believes the school's farm has far more social and economic significance, including introducing students to construction principles when they design and build the farm structures; making the girls better mothers by giving them and their children a new vocabulary to learn and discuss; and making them more conscientious in their food choices. Beyond that, Andrews said, "We have so many kids in Detroit who can't get a job—they're bound for jail, or worse. They could be in charge of their own businesses, small individualistic farms. Adolescent boys especially like to be in charge. Why not encourage them to grow apples here?"

Many conditions have led to the urban agriculture movement: poverty, hunger, climate change, economic and industrial shifts, and even personal tastes and food trends. Many of these issues are discussed and debated in the following chapters: What Is the Purpose of Urban Agriculture? Is Urban Agriculture Economically Sustainable? How Does Urban Agriculture Affect Particular Groups? and What Is the Future of Urban Agriculture? News of tainted food, evolving weather patterns, loss of land to overdevelopment, overcrowded cities, and increasing poverty and hunger have made awareness of this issue an urgent matter. *Opposing Viewpoints: Urban Agriculture* offers a broad examination of this important issue.

OPPOSING
VIEWPOINTS®
SERIES

CHAPTER 1

What Is the Purpose of Urban Agriculture?

Chapter Preface

In 2011 the United States Department of Agriculture (USDA) launched an interactive website called the Food Desert Locator, on which users are able to "get a spatial view of low-income neighborhoods with high concentrations of people who are far from a grocery store." Falling under the umbrella of the federal Healthy Food Financing Initiative (HFFI), which in turn is part of First Lady Michelle Obama's "Let's Move!" program, the Food Desert Locator uses the definition of "food desert" created by the USDA's Economic Research Service 2009 report, *Access to Affordable and Nutritious Food: Measuring and Understanding Food Deserts and Their Consequences; A Report to Congress*. Citing dramatically high rates of obesity, diabetes, heart disease, and malnutrition among poor urban dwellers, the report defined a "food desert" as an "area in the United States with limited access to affordable and nutritious food, particularly such an area composed of predominantly lower-income neighborhoods and communities." While the report did note the difficulty of measuring such notions as "accessibility" and "affordability"—"there is not a widely agreed standard above which an area has 'adequate' access to affordable and nutritious food and below which an area has 'inadequate' access to food"—it concluded unequivocally that food deserts are a genuine problem in American urban and rural areas.

It is taken for granted among many media outlets that poor residents of American cities such as Chicago, Philadelphia, Detroit, and West Oakland (California), must shop for food primarily at liquor stores and gas stations. Other observers have strongly disagreed with this notion, and some even question whether or not food deserts, as they are commonly defined, exist at all. Angie Schmitt wrote in "In Defense of the Corner Market" on *DC.Streetsblog.org* in May 2011, "The argument about food deserts seems to be premised on the assumption that supermarkets—suburban-style, big-box, corporate chain stores with plenty o' parking—are inherently superior to walkable, family-owned food markets that serve low-income populations. The media portrays these corner markets as liquor stores or 'discount' stores carrying little fresh produce and lots of Hostess cupcakes. While there is certainly a class of convenience store that lacks healthy food options, many analyses have completely ignored the presence of small, family-owned food markets and their important role in feeding urban populations."

Further, commentary in the *Economist* in July 2011 questioned the link between poor diet and food deserts altogether, arguing that the presence of a large chain supermarket in a lower-income community has no bearing on what consumers will buy: "Open a full-service supermarket in a food desert and shoppers tend to buy the same artery-clogging junk food as before—they just pay less for it. The unpalatable truth seems to be that some Americans simply do not care to eat a balanced diet, while others, increasingly, cannot afford to. Over the last four years, the price of the healthiest foods has increased at around twice the rate of energy-dense junk food. That is the whole problem, in an organic nutshell." Detroit-based writer James Griffioen brought another perspective to the issue in January 2011: "The myth of a city without supermarkets is hard to kill. . . . Ultimately, that myth perseveres because the mainstream media and its audience is steeped in a suburban mentality where the only grocery stores that really seem to count are those large, big-box chain stores that *are* the only option in so many communities these days, largely because they have put locally-owned and independent stores like the ones you find in Detroit out of business." Whether urban farmers arise because of a lack of healthy foods in their area or just enjoy it, the purpose of urban agriculture is debated by the authors in the following chapter.

| "Livestock keeping in rural niches within fast developing urban areas is a major contributor to monetary income and food security."

Urban Agriculture Helps Create Food Security for Poor Africans

Aldo Lupala and Volker Kreibich

Aldo Lupala is a professor at Ardhi University in Dar es Salaam, Tanzania. Volker Kreibich is a professor at the Universität Dortmund in Dortmund, Germany. In the following viewpoint, Lupala and Kreibich examine the impact of urban livestock keeping in the city of Dar es Salaam, Tanzania. According to the authors, the urban farmers of Dar es Salaam are a diverse group of people, depending upon their demographic identity and how close they live to the city's urban center. But they are united in the sense that they all experience food insecurity to one degree or another. Some of the most successful urban farmers in Dar es Salaam keep poultry, which they use as both a source of nutrition and a source of income, although most poultry farmers in the city use it as a source of income to purchase food for their families. Much of the success of this enterprise, according to the authors, depends on tribal identity, with those involved in the supply chain typically coming from the

Aldo Lupala and Volker Kreibich, "Urban Agriculture—A Key to Food Security?," *Rural 21*, January 2008. Copyright © 2008. All rights reserved. Reproduced by permission.

same region and/or tribal background. Because of the success of the urban poultry business run by formerly impoverished farmers, the city is reorganizing land access, adding community services, and encouraging new business activity.

As you read, consider the following questions:

1. According to the authors, what are the main differences among the livestock keepers of Dar es Salaam?
2. What do Lupala and Kreibich consider to have been a major development in the success of livestock keeping in Dar es Salaam?
3. What are the uniting factors among the urban farmers of Dar es Salaam that have contributed to the success of their agricultural enterprises?

The Tanzanian city of Dar es Salaam now has more than 3.5 million inhabitants. Its population has one of the highest growth rates in urban sub-Saharan Africa, skyrocketing at 7 to 10 percent a year between 1952 and 1992. The peri-urban zone of Dar es Salaam has seen an explosion of population influx from both the inner city and the upcountry rural areas, with growth rates of up to 200 percent in the late 1990s. Urban development has concentrated along the four radial roads, with distinctly rural areas remaining in the interstices [areas between].

The formal sector offers only insufficient employment, so that the majority of urban residents are still engaged in informal activities to sustain their livelihoods. Livestock keeping in rural niches within fast developing urban areas is a major contributor to monetary income and food security. Chronic urban poverty is giving it even more momentum. Livestock keepers in Dar es Salaam are not a homogenous group. They differ in many respects, including the number of animals, landholding, gender, labour and capital input. Also, distances to the urban centre and grazing facilities vary, as do access to animal health services, knowledge of livestock husbandry and transmittances to the rural areas as part of rural-urban linkages.

Nyantira

The settlement of Nyantira is located on the periphery of Dar es Salaam, 18 kilometres south-west of the city centre. Before 1973, only sparsely located homesteads could be found in this area; the land was farmed with crops such as coconuts, cashew nuts and cassava. Today, Nyantira is a good example of successful economic development in a relatively remote peri-urban zone despite a lack of basic community services. An in-depth survey in Nyantira has helped to uncover the strategies which the poor households applied to improve and stabilise their livelihoods through integration into the city-wide economy with livestock keeping.

Cattle breeders from the Kurya tribe immigrated from their homeland at the Kenyan border to Nyantira to establish a foothold in the vicinity of a large city. They took to poultry because the initial investment is moderate and the demand for eggs on the urban market promised quick and sustainable returns. In order to solve the transport problem arising from a location without a motorable road, the settlers called upon young men from their home region who were able to transport 30 egg cartons and more riding bicycles along 15 kilometres of sandy tracks and forest paths to the city.

The poultry is kept indoors in poultry sheds of about 35 square metres that accommodate about 300 chickens. All poultry keepers started by building simple sheds made out of mud and poles and corrugated iron sheets. Within two to three years, most are able to redevelop the structures by replacing wooden poles with concrete and cement blocks for the sub-structure.

Animal feed and vitamins which initially had to be carried from city outlets can now be bought from vending kiosks recently established in Nyantira. The opening of animal feed shops in the settlement marked a major development because poultry feed and medication no longer had to be transported to Nyantira by the egg-ferrying cyclists on their way back home.

Obstacles to Success

The poultry business is doing extremely well. Within just a year or two, the young cyclists are able to acquire plots of land and start breeding their own chickens. The peri-urban economy of the Kurya migrants is thus a striking example of linking rural production locations with urban markets and with the outlying tribal homeland.

Productivity in poultry keeping was initially rather low due to a lack of extension services and poor animal health. Even today, poultry keepers have to take sick chickens over a distance of 14 kilometres to the veterinary service in the city centre.

Access to clean water is ranked as problem number one—not only for animals but also for human consumption. Together with the increasing shortage of affordable plots of land, it has significantly limited the further expansion of the poultry industry in Nyantira despite its success to date.

Like in other areas with peri-urban agriculture, a variety of organisational links have developed with the city in Nyantira in addition to the supply of inputs and services and the marketing of produce. Better-off livestock keepers tend to live in the city centre but keep their livestock at peri-urban locations where local households take care of these animals. The owners in turn provide their workers with free accommodation and cover the costs of medical services.

The Impact on Food Security

Livestock keepers have to apply a wide range of strategies and techniques to cope with market challenges like hampered access to market information, rising transportation costs, or limited flexibility due to inappropriate storage facilities for delicate products. In Nyantira, however, local networks based on kinship ties seem to be working efficiently in informing the egg producers

Global Undernourishment, 2003–05 Versus 1990–92

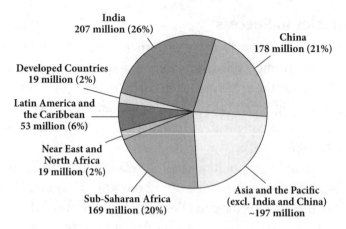

India
207 million (26%)

China
178 million (21%)

Developed Countries
19 million (2%)

Latin America and
the Caribbean
53 million (6%)

Near East and
North Africa
19 million (2%)

Sub-Saharan Africa
169 million (20%)

Asia and the Pacific
(excl. India and China)
~197 million

1990–92
Developing Regions = 823 million
World = 842 million

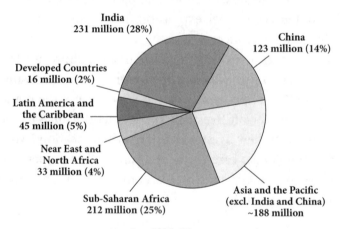

India
231 million (28%)

China
123 million (14%)

Developed Countries
16 million (2%)

Latin America and
the Caribbean
45 million (5%)

Near East and
North Africa
33 million (4%)

Sub-Saharan Africa
212 million (25%)

Asia and the Pacific
(excl. India and China)
~188 million

2003–05
Developing Regions = 832 million
World = 848 million

TAKEN FROM: "Trends in Global Undernourishment," *Urban Agriculture for Sustainable Poverty Alleviation and Food Security*, October 2008.

about changing market determinants and in providing mutual support.

Poultry keeping accounts for a significant improvement in food security, as poor livestock keepers sell livestock products and buy food for their household members. This results in a noticeable nutrition gain in some communities. However, most livestock is mainly kept for commercial purposes and is rarely used for home consumption. In Nyantira, poultry keeping contributes about 90 percent to the household cash income. There, the average monthly income of established poultry breeders is ten times higher than the minimum monthly salary of a government employee in Tanzania. In addition, livestock keeping contributes substantially to food security through extra nutrition for children and family members (15%) and increased purchasing of food (75%). Most households have complemented poultry breeding by vegetable gardening using the same distribution network.

Livestock keeping in peri-urban areas such as Nyantira relies on appropriate local factors, such as affordable land being available, which is the case in low-density areas in the outskirts. Strong organisational links between livestock owners, labourers and egg-ferrying cyclists within the poultry value chain which are based on their common origin in the same rural region and their tribal identity represent a highly supportive factor. This asset allows them to make use of the multiple benefits peri-urban livestock keeping offers, including access to land, the ability to feed the households involved as part of the rapidly growing urban population, continuity of employment, accumulation of capital, and improved housing.

New and Existing Support Systems

Although Nyantira has only had poor access to socio-economic services so far, its growth is motivated by the availability of consumer goods. The market networks with backward and forward commodity flows facilitated by the daily interactions between

Nyantira and the city provide up-to-date information. The high profits achieved stimulate the growth of the settlement through the increase of existing enterprises and the establishment of new ones. As a result, the population is growing rapidly, land use patterns are changing and local initiatives to buy land for community services are increasing. In order to cope with the demand for land, more plots have been parcelled. The transformation of a poor subsistence economy to commercial poultry and gardening represents a new practice in peri-urban land use change.

In the Nyantira case, poultry and gardening have emerged as profitable urban land uses based on strong social cohesion among the immigrants and with their home people. Their socially crafted institutions provided the bottom line of the economic and social success of the Nyantira community in the absence of extension services and any other state intervention. The importance of social capital can be only partially substituted by capacity building in running economic activities, particularly poultry, gardening, horticulture, floriculture and dairy, although tailor-made training will enable peri-urban farmers to compete more effectively on urban markets.

| "*Urban agriculture . . . reduces pressure on low-income residents' limited family budgets while increasing the intake of much needed fresh fruits and vegetables.*"

Urban Agriculture Helps Create Food Security for Poor Americans

Nina Haletky and Owen Taylor

Nina Haletky graduated from the Urban Studies program at San Francisco State University and currently works as Community Outreach Coordinator at GreenCitizen. Owen Taylor has a degree in Urban Studies from San Francisco State University and is employed as City Farms Program Manager at the organization Just Food in New York City. The authors, in the following viewpoint, consider the role of food systems in increasing access to fresh food by low-income urban dwellers, arguing that, while many large American cities have addressed the problem of food insecurity by offering access to food through charitable groups such as food banks and other "hunger relief networks," this method is overly dependent on a corporate-directed, industrial food system that offers too many processed foods and fails to offer any economic stimulation to cities. By contrast, a planned system of sustainable farming that is built into a city's core plan, alongside housing, transportation, and economic development, Haletky and Taylor assert, would allow lower-income city residents to gain regular access to healthier food as well as including those residents in a wider plan involving moving toward environmental sustainability, rescuing vacant areas from urban blight, and engaging in entrepreneurial farming activities, from growing to selling fresh produce.

As you read, consider the following questions:

1. What is the current process of global corporate food production called, according to the authors?
2. According to Haletky and Taylor, what is the definition of "food security"?
3. What are some of the populations that the authors argue have benefited from job training at urban farming programs?

A food system is defined [by urban planners Kameshwari Pothukuchi and Jerome L. Kaufman] as a "chain of activities connecting food production, processing, distribution, consumption, and waste management, as well as all the associated regulatory institutions and activities." Unfortunately the planning field does not currently value food systems planning as much as other areas of planning, such as housing or transportation. A revealing study conducted by . . . Pothukuchi and Kaufman in which twenty-two planning agencies were surveyed, reveals low levels of involvement in food planning for the following perceived reasons: food issues are not in the realm of the urban built environment, food issues are driven primarily by the private market, there is insufficient federal funding, and a lack of knowledge about food systems.

A Lack of Food Planning

The planning profession [assert Pothukuchi and Kaufman] "lays claim to being comprehensive in scope, future-oriented, and public interest driven, and of wanting to enhance the livability of human settlements." Planners are in unique positions of power to mediate the connections between the different stakeholders in a food system. They are trained to analyze the interconnectedness of systems in cities and understand communities as a whole. This implication of interconnectedness "should lead planners directly to a concern about food systems, as the food system is so intricately connected to the land and land use and so central to health and the goal of improving human settlements" [states Raquel Pinderhughes]. Pothukuchi and Kaufman give many practical reasons why food systems should be integral to the planning field's scope, including (but certainly not limited to), the important role food plays in the local economy; high employment in the food sector and the significant amount of income spent on food; housing costs competing with food purchasing power; as well as public health concerns.

Fortunately planners are taking notice—in the last few years, food system planning has appeared as a featured theme at major planners conferences such as the American Planning Association conference and the Association of Collegiate Schools of Planning conference. Many cities and states have established food policy councils that have begun to address the food issues in many U.S. cities, so the future looks hopeful for incorporating food planning into government agendas.

American Food Insecurity

Over the past several decades food production, processing and distribution has grown more concentrated in the hands of a few global corporate powers in a process known as vertical integration. Increasingly, small regional and local farms find it impossible to compete in the global industrialized food system dominated by the "free" market. Large scale, industrial agriculture is characterized by high yields, productivity, efficiency and the domination of the food system through mass production of raw agricultural materials, centralized control over the processing, distributing, marketing, as well as import and export of food over vast distance. Despite the high yields and great abundance of the food supply, 10% of all households in the United States (approximately 33 million people) go hungry on a regular basis.

In particular, low-income urban communities (disproportionately communities of color) are especially devastated by inadequate access to fresh, healthy food. This is due to many factors including insufficient food planning, food industry consolidation, the closing of large-scale supermarkets and subsequent "supermarket redlining" in low-income urban areas, and poor access to transportation. This leads to a dependence on fast food restaurants and small neighborhood convenience stores and markets which tend to have higher prices and considerably more processed and less healthy food options than their large scale grocery store counterparts in higher-income areas. These limited food options create patterns of hunger and poor nutrition and result in illnesses and diseases such as obesity, diabetes, hypertension, heart failure, strokes, and various forms of cancer. To address the food insecurity issues in low-income urban areas a significant hunger relief network has been developed including food banks, food pantries, produce gleaning operations, and surplus commodity distribution. However, this network tends to rely upon the corporate dominated food system and still leaves wide gaps in food security.

Food security can be defined as all persons living in a community at all times having access to safe, culturally acceptable, nutritionally adequate food through a local, sustainable, self-reliant, socially just, non-emergency food system. A food secure city should emphasize local sources of production and processing within a food system that supports economic and environmental sustainability but focuses primarily on creating food access, especially for low-income people. "Community food security cannot be expected to solve all the ills emerging from the current global food system," nor "is it intended as a replacement for federal entitlement programs aimed at poor and vulnerable residents" [states Pothukuchi]. Instead it aims to fill the gaps that these current paths for food production and distribution neglect and offers an alternative approach that supplements and strengthens a local food system.

Opportunities for Urban Agriculture

Urban Agriculture involves the growing of crops and/or livestock within urban areas or at their periphery. Urban agriculture is a key component to developing a sustainable community food system, and if planned properly, can alleviate many of the problems of food insecurity. The Community Food Security Coalition (CFSC) maintains a committee whose "primary purpose is to utilize urban agriculture as a means for the food insecure to gain access to fresh, affordable, nutritious food" [note the coalition's Katherine H. Brown and Anne Carter]. The existence of this national committee represents a growing movement in the planning field, which asserts that urban agriculture is essential for maintaining healthy, food secure cities.

While urban agriculture is central to the lives of hundreds of millions of people throughout the world, in the United States planning and policy arena, "very little emphasis has been placed on the role that a well-planned, well-supported, urban agricultural sector can play in reducing poverty, food insecurity, and waste in cities" [asserts Pinderhughes]. A city's ability to feed itself is a valuable component of sustainable development. As the global food economy becomes further and further removed from life in cities, the opportunity is ripe for cities to encourage urban agriculture—an activity that alleviates food injustices by increasing access to healthy food and simultaneously improves many other economic, social, and environmental conditions.

The Benefits of Urban Agriculture

Urban agriculture brings numerous benefits to communities in which it is sown and nurtured. An initial goal for this research was to focus on the economic viability of urban agriculture. However, when measuring economic successes from entrepreneurial agriculture endeavors alone, the profits are modest at best and self-sufficiency is low. To accurately capture the development potential of urban gardening, the possibility for building social capital must be acknowledged. There still however remains a need for proving the economic viability to funders and policy-makers, who remain under the influence of traditional economic development standards. While it is possible to provide these economic benefits, disseminating the multiple benefits of urban agriculture as a whole can be a highly effective advocating strategy.

Urban agriculture's economic benefits include increased economic vitality from the start-up of local entrepreneurial businesses, additional community investment from local food sales, and job training and employment. Food makes up a significant portion of a local economy (generally about 20% of retail sales and 20% of service jobs), and as over 90% of the West Oakland purchasing power is spent outside of the area, there is great potential for the growth of a local food economy through entrepreneurial urban agriculture projects. Growing niche products, such as mixed greens for restaurants, can help financially sustain a program and fund community-based projects.

Urban agriculture can provide an important, relatively affordable source of fresh, nutritious produce. This reduces pressure on low-income residents' limited family budgets while increasing the intake of much needed fresh fruits and vegetables. Between 15 and 30% of household budgets are spent on food. However, while food budgets are elastic compared to more rigid expenses such as rent, the poorest families must often make the terrible choice between paying rent and eating adequately and healthfully. The food money saved by growing food can be invested in other areas of the local economy. A study by the Philadelphia Urban Gardening Project found that low-income people who garden each save an average of $150 in food costs per growing season. Most ate fresh produce 5 months of the year, preserved some for off-season consumption, and shared their produce with friends, family, neighbors and community organizations.

In communities with high rates of joblessness and under-employment, urban gardens and farms have proved to be excellent vehicles for job training, and have been effective in providing programs for marginalized youth and adults. Berkeley Youth Alternatives (BYA) runs a half-acre garden in West Berkeley, California, and offers training to low-income teens who earn $6/hr working 15 to 20 hours per week during the school year, and 20–30 hours per week in the summer. The All People's Garden, founded in 1978 in Manhattan, runs a program for juvenile first-time offenders, a teen drug prevention project, a HeadStart program for 4- to 12-year-olds, and a program that connects youth with local artists. Other programs have had highly successful rehabilitation efforts through providing jobs and job training to prisoner, homeless and substance abuse populations.

Urban Agriculture Can Reduce Crime

Community involvement in neighborhood revitalization through urban agriculture prevents violence, provides remediation of blighted property and fosters community empowerment. Lack of green space is considered one of the most significant problems leading to unrest and crime. Gardens are a source of pride, community cohesion and local leadership in the face of the toxic vacant lots and lack of services that come with disinvestment and ghettoization. During the L.A. riots in 1992, the areas around the community gardens remarkably escaped destruction. Burglaries and thefts in the vicinity of a newly created community garden in Philadelphia plummeted from about forty incidents per month to four. A new garden in the Mission District of San Francisco led to the formation of a Neighborhood Watch group, which made the area unattractive to drug dealers. There was a 28% drop in crime around the garden after the first year.

The use of urban agriculture for greening blighted vacant lots proves to be highly effective. In the Mission District of San Francisco, Parque Niños Unidos and Treat Commons Community Garden were built on a formerly toxic vacant lot which housed drug users and served illegally as place to dump trash. As there was no other nearby green space, children were using this lot as a play space. It is now a safe and beautiful place to gather, play and garden. The City of Chicago, recognizing the power of urban gardening to relieve blight, has established Greencorps, a strong citywide greening program in which qualified community groups are given workshops, soil amendments, tools, plants, and other materials to conduct landscaping and gardening projects on vacant land.

Other environmental benefits include the improvement of human and environmental health through the use of local sustainable production and processing techniques. As prime farmland in the U.S. is consumed by sprawl at dramatic rates, we rely more and more upon imported mass produced food. "Food products typically travel between 1,500 and 2,500 miles from farm to plate," [state Brown and Carter]. The practices of industrial agriculture result in massive environmental degradation. The heavy use of chemicals and pesticides leads to the depletion and contamination of surface water, groundwater and soil and causes air pollution and serious health risks for farm workers and surrounding communities. When carefully planned and skillfully applied, certain urban agriculture techniques can provide impressive yields using very little space, reducing the strain on land and water resources. Also, the possibility for food to reach a consumer the same day that it is harvested challenges the fuel-dependent conventional food system. When managed properly, composting and reuse of waste water for urban agriculture can significantly decrease the amount of solid and liquid waste in a city.

Despite the immense potential of urban agriculture to stimulate the local economy, alleviate food insecurity, revitalize blighted areas and provide an alternative sustainable approach to destructive industrial agricultural practices, negative perceptions and lack of awareness has created obstacles to growing food in U.S. cities. With proper support and planning through collaboration between private, community and government interests, a new movement towards food secure cities can be realized.

> "The work of involving people in
> producing and distributing healthy
> food . . . is part of equalizing power in
> American Society."

Urban Agriculture Feeds and Empowers People

Roger Bybee

Roger Bybee is an activist and writer in Milwaukee, Wisconsin. In the following viewpoint, he profiles the agricultural business venture of former professional basketball player and MacArthur Foundation "genius grant" winner Will Allen, whose urban agriculture project, Growing Power, has a staff of thirty-five employees at its base of operations in Milwaukee. Additionally, according to Bybee, Allen has created a farming cooperative with about three hundred family farms in Wisconsin, Illinois, Michigan, and several southern states to deliver fresh produce to city-dwellers year-round. Bybee writes that Growing Power recruits area young people for its Youth Corps program, where they learn about agriculture and running a farm. Allen's success, Bybee asserts, comes largely from his organization's integration into the community it serves, particularly the job training and employment opportunities it provides, through which Allen addresses his community's ongoing food security issues.

As you read, consider the following questions:
1. How does Bybee say Allen describes his family's reputation during his childhood?
2. What does Allen farm other than vegetables, according to the author?
3. How many people from around the world does Bybee say participate in Growing Power's formal training sessions?

A t the northern outskirts of Milwaukee, in a neighborhood of boxy post-WWII [World War II] homes near the sprawling Park Lawn housing project, stand 14 greenhouses arrayed on two acres of land. This is Growing Power, the only land within the Milwaukee city limits zoned as farmland.

Founded by MacArthur Foundation "genius" fellow Will Allen, Growing Power is an active farm producing tons of food each year, a food distribution hub, and a training center. It's also the home base for an expanding network of similar community food centers, including a Chicago branch run by Allen's daughter, Erika. Growing Power is in what Allen calls a "food desert," a part of the city devoid of full-service grocery stores but lined with fast-food joints, liquor stores, and convenience stores selling mostly soda and sweets. Growing Power is an oasis in that desert.

Roots in Farming

Allen's parents were sharecroppers in South Carolina until they bought the small farm in Rockville, Maryland, where Allen grew up. "My parents were the biggest influence on my life," says Allen. "We didn't have a TV and we relied on a wood stove, but we were known as the 'food family' because we had so much food. We could feed 30 people for supper."

He was a high school All-American in basketball, played for the University of Miami, and played pro ball with the American Basketball Association in Europe. At a towering 6 feet 7 inches, with [Arnold] Schwarzenegger–size biceps, and chiseled features, Allen looks ready to step back onto the court.

After stints as an executive for Kentucky Fried Chicken and Proctor and Gamble, he returned to his family roots. "I never wanted a career in the corporate world, but I wanted to be able to afford a good education for my kids," he explains. "At the right time, the kids were in college and the opportunity to buy the farm and start Growing Power came up," Allen remembers. "From a spiritual standpoint, it worked out right; it was a natural thing, something I wanted to do."

Growing Food

Since 1993, Allen has focused on developing Growing Power's urban agriculture project, which grows vegetables and fruit in its greenhouses, raises goats, ducks, bees, turkeys, and—in an aquaponics [fish-farming] system designed by Allen—tilapia and Great Lakes Perch—altogether, 159 varieties of food.

Growing Power also has a 40-acre rural farm in Merton, 45 minutes outside Milwaukee, with five acres devoted to intensive vegetable growing and the balance used for sustainably grown hays, grasses, and legumes which provide food for the urban farm's livestock.

Allen has taken the knowledge he gained growing up on the farm and supplemented it with the latest in sustainable techniques and his own experimentation.

Growing Power composts more than 6 million pounds of food waste a year, including the farm's own waste, material from local food distributors, spent grain from a local brewery, and the grounds from a local coffee shop. Allen counts as part of his livestock the red wiggler worms that turn that waste into "Milwaukee Black Gold" worm castings.

Allen seems to take a particular delight in thrusting his steam-shovel-sized hands into a rich mixture of soil and worms in Growing Power's greenhouses. "You can't grow anything without good soil," he preaches to a group touring the project.

Allen designed an aquaponics system, built for just $3,000, a fraction of the $50,000 cost of a commercially-built system. In addition to tilapia, a common fish in aquaculture, Allen also grows yellow perch, a fish once a staple of the Milwaukee diet. Pollution and overfishing killed the Lake Michigan perch fishery; Growing Power will soon make this local favorite available again. The fish are raised in 10,000-gallon tanks where 10,000 fingerlings grow to market size in as little as nine months.

A Vertical Growing System

But the fish are only one product of Allen's aquaponics system. The water from the fish tanks flows into a gravel bed, where the waste breaks down to produce nitrogen in a form plants can use. The gravel bed supports a crop of watercress, which further filters the water. The nutrient-rich water is then pumped to overhead beds to feed crops of tomatoes and salad greens.

The plants extract the nutrients while the worms in the soil consume bacteria from the water, which emerges virtually pristine and flows back into the fish tanks. This vertical growing system multiplies the productivity of the farm's limited space.

"Growing Power is probably the leading urban agricultural project in the United States," says Jerry Kaufman, a professor emeritus in urban and regional planning at the University of Wisconsin–Madison. "Growing Power is not just talking about what needs to be changed, it's accomplishing it."

Growing Community

Simply growing that much food in a small space is a remarkable achievement. But it's only the start of Growing Power's mission. "Low-quality food is resulting in diabetes, obesity, and sickness from processed food," Allen maintains. "Poor people are not educated about nutrition and don't have access to stores that sell nutritious food, and they wind up with diabetes and heart disease."

Growing healthy food is part of a larger transformational project that will create a more just society, as Allen sees it.

He also works on the Growing Food and Justice Initiative, a national network of about 500 people that fights what he calls "food racism," the structural denial of wholesome food to poor African-American and Latino neighborhoods. "One of our four strategic goals is to dismantle racism in the food system. Just as there is redlining in lending, there is redlining by grocery stores, denying access to people of color by staying out of minority communities."

Selling a Healthy Lifestyle

The store at Growing Power's Milwaukee farm is the only place for miles around that carries fresh produce, free-range eggs, grass-fed beef, and homegrown honey. Even in winter, customers find the handmade shelves and aging coolers stocked with fresh-picked salad greens.

Growing Power co-director Karen Parker, who has worked alongside Allen since the project started, says, "It's a wonderful thing to change people's lives through changing what they're eating." Parker believes her parents would have lived much longer with a healthier diet. She takes a deep pride in providing fresh, healthy food. "Last summer during the salmonella problem with tomatoes, I was able to tell customers, 'You don't have to worry. These tomatoes were grown right here.' I found myself selling out of tomatoes."

Growing Power supplements its own products with food from the Rainbow Farming Cooperative, which Allen started at the same time as Growing Power.

The cooperative is made up of about 300 family farms in Wisconsin, Michigan, Northern Illinois, and the South. The southern farmers, who are primarily African-Americans, make it possible to offer fresh fruits and vegetables year-round. The produce goes into Growing Power's popular Farm-to-City Market Baskets. A week's worth of 12–15 varieties of produce costs $16. A $9 "Junior/Senior" basket, with smaller quantities of the same produce, is also available.

Each Friday, Growing Power delivers 275–350 Market Baskets of food to more than 20 agencies, community centers, and other sites around Milwaukee for distribution. Bernita Samson, a retiree in her 60s with eight grandchildren, picked up the Market Basket habit from her brother and late mother. "I get the biggest kick out of what I get in my bag each week," she says. "At Sunday dinners my grandkids say, 'Ooh, Grandma this is good!' They really like what they call the 'smashed potatoes.'"

For Samson, Growing Power provides not only healthy food but also a vital source of community. "Sometimes it's so crowded at the [Growing Power] store on Saturdays you can't even get up in there. Going there gives you a chance to meet people and talk."

Creating Jobs

Growing Power is also a source of 35 good-paying jobs in an area of high unemployment. The staff of Growing Power is highly diverse—a mixture of young and old, African-American, white, Asian, Native American, and Latino, with remarkably varied work histories. All live nearby. Co-director Karen Parker, a high-energy African-American woman who radiates warmth whether greeting her 6-year-old granddaughter or welcoming a volunteer, notes that some staff are former professionals who left the high-stress environments of corporations, social work, and other fields. At Growing Power they find a new kind of fulfillment in the blend of hard physical labor and thoughtful planning based on scientific research. Others are former blue-collar workers, farmers, or recent college graduates. All find satisfaction in transforming how Americans eat.

Loretta Mays, 21, who works in the marketing department, was only 14 when Karen Parker recruited her into the Growing Power Youth Corps program. "It's a good learning experience, and you learn the importance of good food. I never understood how food was grown. Now, it's like, 'Wow, I can grow my own garden.'"

Blaming the Poor for Food Insecurity Worsens the Problem

Blaming food insecurity and hunger on poverty [essentially, inability to earn sufficient cash to buy food] has been the official position of most governments and of international institutions like UN-FAO [United Nations Food and Agriculture Organization], World Bank, IMF [International Monetary Fund], and CGIAR [Consultative Group on International Agricultural Research]. Unfortunately such notions serve powerful economic and political interests that perpetuate hunger, malnutrition, diseases, illiteracy, ignorance, urban slums and filth and rural poverty globally.

Arun Shrivastava, "Poverty and Food Insecurity in the Developing World," Global Research, *May 7, 2009.*

Growing Youth

Four middle and high schools bring students to Growing Power to learn about vermiculture (raising worms) and growing crops, and to eat the food they've grown. The impact can change the kids' lives.

Anthony Jackson started working at Growing Power when he was 14, with half of his earnings going to school clothes and half to a bank account that his church set up. At age 20, he went away to college.

"I learned a good work ethic—that things don't come easy," he says of his time at Growing Power. "You'd see Will doing the same things he asked you to do."

The experience helped to shape the direction of his college education. "Early on, the importance of the healthy food really didn't hit home," he says. "But when I got a degree in natural resources, it came to mean a lot more." Jackson, now 29, still maintains a strong connection, shopping at Growing Power and attending workshops.

Working with the young people in the community is central to Growing Power's work and its hopes for the future. It provides year-round gardening activities for kids aged 10–18 at its Milwaukee headquarters and offers summertime farming experience on its parcel in Merton, adjacent to the Boys and Girls Club's Camp Mason. Growing Power recently leased five acres at Milwaukee's Maple Tree School and built a community garden in partnership with the school. Growing Power also assists school gardens at the Urban Day School and the University School of Milwaukee.

"For kids to make their own soil, grow their own food, and then get to eat it, that's a very powerful experience," Will Allen says. "There's nothing like hands-on experience for kids who are bored with school. They get excited about what they're learning and then take it back to their classes."

Growing Power on the Road

Success in Milwaukee isn't enough for Allen. Growing Power seeks nothing less than, in the words of the organization's mission statement, "creating a just world, one food-secure community at a time." To show that the techniques pioneered in Milwaukee can work anywhere, Growing Power is helping set up five projects in impoverished areas across the United States, including training centers in Forest City, Arkansas; Lancaster, Massachusetts; and Shelby and Mound Bayou, Mississippi.

The largest application of Growing Power's model is in Chicago, where Erika Allen, Will's daughter, is carrying on the family tradition. The Chicago project started in the Cabrini-Green public housing project, where Growing Power's techniques helped the Fourth Presbyterian Church transform a basketball court into a flourishing community garden fueled by Will Allen's beloved red worms. Growing Power also has a half-acre farm in

Grant Park, in the heart of downtown Chicago. The Grant Park project focuses on job training for young people, involving them in all aspects of growing the 150 varieties of heirloom vegetables, herbs, and edible flowers the farm sells in Chicago farmers markets and through the Farm-to-City Market Basket program, like the one pioneered in Milwaukee.

After Erika Allen, 39, earned a degree in art therapy, she eventually settled back into her family's farming tradition, which she believes extends back some 400 years. "I was very much influenced by that tradition, and I got really inspired," she says. "It was a way of learning to honor my ancestors."

But she has not turned her back on her artistic impulses. "With my love of art, the Grant Park project is an opportunity to integrate the two—with the colors, design, textures of the plants."

The most important element, she says, is "to see it inspiring other people. When people in communities like Detroit are really suffering, we can show that we did it in Chicago, with women and a bunch of teenagers."

Seeking Justice Through Food

The work of involving people in producing and distributing healthy food in Chicago's food deserts is part of equalizing power in American society, Erika Allen says. "Our work is infused with social justice, fighting racism and oppression."

The same hunger for justice drives Will Allen's vision of changing the food system. "How do you take our model and our vision around the world?" Allen asks. "It takes some footsoldiers who become change agents. We've trained an awful lot of people."

Every year, 10,000 people tour the Growing Power farms. About 3,000 youths and adults from around the world participate in formal training sessions, learning how to build aquaponics systems, construct "hoop houses" (low-cost greenhouses covered by clear plastic), use compost to heat greenhouses, use worms to turn waste into rich fertilizer, and all the other low-tech, high-yield techniques that Growing Power has developed or adapted.

Will Allen takes obvious pleasure in seeing people fed healthy food in great quantities, just as his parents did on their small farm. But he says he derives his deepest satisfaction from a sense of changing the lives of other people harmed by the present food system and the inequities it reflects. "I don't do things to satisfy myself," he states firmly. "This is what I'm doing for a bigger pool of people out there."

*"Sustainable, local food systems are
not only a way to ensure food security
but also a means of addressing social
justice issues."*

Urban Agriculture Is Really About Social Justice

Phoebe Connelly and Chelsea Ross

Phoebe Connelly is former managing editor of In These Times *and web editor at* American Prospect. *Chelsea Ross is a Chicago-based writer. In the following viewpoint, the authors discuss access to safe, healthy food as a social justice issue, noting that low-income urban residents tend to be people of color, many of whom have considerably higher rates of illness and obesity than their wealthier counterparts. Connelly and Ross assert that with their proximity to chain grocery stores often prohibitively distant and little or no reliable transportation available, poor urban dwellers are effectively denied access to healthy foods and forced to buy food at liquor stores and convenience marts in walking distance. According to the authors, urban agriculture counters the nutritional dangers and social injustice of these "food deserts" by "optimizing the amount of food grown on the least amount of land." With smaller plots and fewer resources, the authors explain, urban gardeners must put their land to the best possible use and waste little time getting their pro-*

duce to consumers, either through farmers' markets or home delivery. Funding is the biggest obstacle to urban farming, according to Connelly and Ross. The farm bill passed by the US Congress in 2007 subsidizes the meat and dairy industries while offering little to growers of produce, the authors declare, and in order to address the problem of food security in poor communities, urban farmers must keep their prices low to ensure affordability.

As you read, consider the following questions:

1. According to the authors, what are women who live in food-insecure areas more prone to develop?
2. What, according to Andy Fisher, is the only fruit or vegetable subsidized in the farm bill?
3. What, according to Connelly and Ross, is one of the primary ways to ensure sustainability?

The Food Project is part of a growing urban agriculture movement to improve access to quality food in cities by creating local sources of fresh produce. The movement is showing that sustainable, local food systems are not only a way to ensure food security but also a means of addressing social justice issues. . . .

"The biggest crisis in our food system is the lack of access to good, healthy, fresh food, for people living in cities, particularly in low-income communities," says Anna Lappé, co-founder with her mother Frances Moore Lappé of the Small Planet Institute. "Urban agriculture work is one of the most powerful solutions, because it brings food directly into the communities." . . .

A Growing Enterprise

The Food Project began on Ward Cheney's farm in Lincoln, Mass., about 24 miles west of Boston, with the goal of strengthening young people's connection to the land. They started by busing city kids out to the country, but the group now farms five urban plots—a total of 2.5 acres. Each summer the Food Project employs 60 kids to work on both the urban and rural farms. After the summer, the youth can return as interns to learn how to run the project's farmers' markets and commercial kitchen.

In the Midwest, Growing Power runs three farms in Chicago, youth employment and education programs and a world famous vermiculture (worm compost) project.

In Oakland, Calif., People's Grocery operates five urban gardens in the largely black and Latino communities of West and North Oakland, as well as a youth nutrition program staffed by young people.

In Brooklyn, Added Value has turned an old asphalt baseball diamond into a full-functioning farm. And in Philadelphia, Mill Creek Farm is using storm runoff to irrigate its urban farm. Indeed, community agriculture projects are sprouting up in cities across the country—in San Francisco (Alemany Farm), Buffalo (Massachusetts Avenue Project), Birmingham, Ala. (Jones Valley Urban Farm), and Houston (Urban Harvest). According to the USDA [US Department of Agriculture], the number of farmers' markets has grown by 50 percent since 1994, and the federal Community Food Projects Competitive Grant Program is funding more than twice as many groups as it did a decade ago.

Beyond Organic

The organic food movement is rapidly changing how America eats and grows its food. Between 1997 and 2001, farmers added a million acres of certified organic land, doubling the amount of organic pasture and more than doubling organic cropland. This reflects not just a rise of specialty retailers like Whole Foods. By 2003 organic products could be found in 73 percent of conventional grocery stores according to a USDA study, and last summer [2006], the retail giant Wal-Mart began selling organics. But Erika Allen, development director of Growing Power, says the organic label doesn't tell the whole story. "There are organic farmers on the walls of Whole Foods who have some atrocious labor practices—atrocious. They're just like plantation owners. People don't know that."

Moreover, organic food is still largely inaccessible to low-income communities and communities of color. And the costs associated with being certified organic have led many urban agriculture programs to shy away from being certified. "We are what most folks would consider organic, but we're not certified," the Food Project's [Robert] Burns says. "That's not as important to us. We're in the community; folks can just come by and see our practices. It's about transparency."

Accessibility is at the heart of what these groups call food security. "It's about everyone having access to culturally appropriate and nutritional food at all times," says Danielle Andrews, who heads up farming for Food Project's Dorchester plots.

"We're using food to make social connections," says Growing Power's Allen. "It's not just about growing food—it's about practices and how people form relationships, get comfortable with each other and learn to communicate through really owning the food system."

Forming such sustainable relationships inherently requires addressing issues of privilege. Growing Power manages a farm on the edge of Cabrini Green, Chicago's most notorious housing project. The site is owned by Fourth Presbyterian Church, one of the wealthiest congregations in the city. "The work that we're doing is social justice work," says Allen, who is bi-racial. "For white folks to support and ally with people of color and communities that are struggling, they have to understand that it's not just about knowing how to grow lettuce. It's important that people doing these projects are very transparent about why they're there."

Oases in the Food Desert

In West Oakland, home to City Slicker and People's Grocery, liquor stores outnumber grocery stores 40 to one. The most readily available food is fried. On the other side of the country, in Added Value's Brooklyn neighborhood, the last grocery store shut its doors in 2001. Federal studies classify such communities as "food insecure," but they are popularly known as "food deserts." A study in the June 2001 *Journal of Nutrition* found that women living in "food insecure" areas were more likely to be overweight and thus at risk for obesity-related illnesses like diabetes and heart disease.

To counter the harm caused by food deserts, urban agriculture focuses on high-density food production—optimizing the amount of food grown on the least amount of land. City Slicker grew 6,500 pounds of produce last year on less than one acre of land. "If the average person eats three to four hundred pounds of produce per year, that doesn't feed that many people," says City Slicker's [founder Willow] Rosenthal. "But I'm not saying it's insignificant, because those couple dozen people improved their diet."

These projects also help people sustain themselves. Both City Slicker and Food Project run backyard gardening programs that provide lead testing to determine the safety of soil, wooden planters, seeds, seedlings and ongoing assistance for the life of the garden.

"Our backyard garden program fits with the idea that the human resources are here, what's lacking are the materials," says Rosenthal. "There are folks coming to us in their 20s and 40s saying, 'I really want to know how to do this. I remember farming when I was five with my grandmother.'"

Encouraging Backyard Gardening

Since the program's inception in 2005, City Slicker has helped build 50 backyard gardens and has set a goal of 50 per year in the future. "We're building a whole community of urban gardeners," says Rosenthal.

Two years ago [in 2005], City Slicker helped Shirley Chunn start a garden. What started as two boxes has now taken over her yard. "It's really nice to just go out and relax in the morning and see all my vegetables," says Chunn. Four of her neighbors now have City Slicker gardens.

According to City Slicker, 40 percent of the 2006 participants were able to grow half or more of their household's produce, 30 percent experienced a positive change in their health, and 50 percent added more fresh vegetables to their diet. City Slicker also buys excess produce from these backyard gardens at a premium organic rate, which it then sells at a lower price at its community farm stand.

The economics—whether through production or backyard programs—are not insignificant. In its primer on urban agriculture the CFSC writes, "Maintaining regional and local farm-to-consumer enterprises helps keep the entire industry accountable for the food system, increasing the likelihood that food is produced and consumed in sustainable ways." The CFSC [Community Food Security Coalition] cites the Maine Organic Farmers and Gardeners Association, which estimates that if every family in Maine spent $10 a week on local food, $104 million would be kept in the local economy.

Cultivating Leaders

Four years ago [in 2003], Geralina Fortier, then 17, got involved with People's Grocery to fulfill a high school community service requirement. Today, Fortier coordinates People's youth nutrition programs. "We believe that youth are the best agents for change, especially to one another, so we create workshops and presentations about eating healthy," says Fortier, as she shovels compost onto a new bed at People's 55th Street garden in West Oakland.

Now a college student majoring in community and health education, Fortier says her work with People's Grocery has changed her life. Asked what she would be doing if she hadn't gotten involved with People's Grocery, she replies, "I'd be fat."

"I'm pretty radical about my diet," says Fortier, "A lot of my friends thought I was crazy and still do." After three years as a strict vegan, she recently switched to a raw food diet because "that's how we should be eating anyway."

At Brooklyn's Added Value, the conversation about nutrition starts in grade school. Almost every child in the local school district has visited the farm at least once through its "Farm to School" program. Added Value also runs a youth program that teaches high school kids food production and sales, media literacy, sustainable business development and community education and organizing.

"We're not growing farmers, we're trying to grow young people who are inspired by the world around them and who care and see themselves as empowered to take action in fixing things," says Caroline Loomis, Added Value's community education coordinator. . . .

A Food and Not a Farm Bill

Andy Fisher is one of the founders of the CFSC, which formed in 1994 to lobby for changes in the 1996 [farm] bill. For Fisher and others wanting to transform food access and production in the United States, changing what the government funds in the farm bill is crucial. "You've got a structure of commodity programs subsidizing—corn, dairy and meat—to the exclusion of other crops," says Fisher. "Take the food pyramid: The farm bill subsidizes the exact opposite of that: 72 percent of all farm subsidies are going into dairy and meat production and smaller amounts into grains for human consumption. The only fruits or vegetables subsidized are apples. So there is a real impact on people's diets. In a very broad sense the farm bill is a food bill, and should be thought of that way."

In addition to subsidizing Big Ag, the farm bill allocates funds for the food stamp program, which, as the nation's largest nutrition program, has a significant impact on consumption patterns. In 2006, 26.7 million Americans received food stamps.

The version of the farm bill passed in the House this summer [2007] has expanded funding to encourage food stamp recipients to shop at farmers' markets: $32 million is allocated to

US Food Insecurity on the Rise

In 2008, 85.4 percent of U.S. households were food secure throughout the year. Food-secure households had consistent access to enough food for active healthy lives for all household members at all times during the year. The remaining 14.6 percent (17 million households) were food insecure. These households, at some time during the year, had difficulty providing enough food for all their members due to a lack of resources. The prevalence of food insecurity was up from 11.1 percent (13 million households) in 2007 and was the highest observed since nationally representative food security surveys were initiated in 1995.

Mark Nord, Margaret Andrews, and Steven Carlson, Household Food Security in the United States, *Economic Research Report Number 83, USDA, November 2009.*

the renamed Farmers' Market Promotion Program; also the bill expands both who is eligible to sell at markets, and the availability of Electronic Benefit Transfer technology to process food stamps as payment. A 2004 UCLA [University of California at Los Angeles] study by researchers at the School of Public Health found that offering those receiving government food assistance (in this case, the Women, Infants and Children program) access to farmers' markets resulted in increased fruit and vegetable consumption that continued beyond the offered incentive.

The House version of the farm bill also allocates $30 million over the next five years to the Community Food Projects [CFP] Competitive Grants Program, which, since its inception in 1996, has funded 240 programs to help low-income communities meet their nutritional needs. (The Food Project and Growing

Power have received three grants each.) Stephanie Larsen, policy organizer with the CFSC cautions, however, that in the 2007 bill CFP funds were changed from mandatory (that is, guaranteed at that level each year) to discretionary (subject to the annual budget approval). "Due to the nature of the appropriations process, there is always a significant possibility that CFP will get much less than $30 million a year and we would have to fight for it annually against all other programs."

It remains to be seen what will happen in the Senate, but legislators are starting to realize the importance of urban agriculture funding. "I rise today to express my support for the [farm bill] . . . but also to express my concern about the lack of funding for community food projects," said Rep. Rush Holt (D-N.J.) on the House floor.

Owning What You Till

The 2007 farm bill may help urban agriculture, but larger questions about sustainability remain. "No one is against gardening," says [University of Illinois landscape architecture professor Laura] Lawson, "but not everyone wants to fund it."

The massive federal subsidies received by Big Ag companies help keep food prices artificially low. That means small-scale, sustainable agriculture must self-subsidize its prices to compete in the marketplace. And as the profile of urban agriculture rises, urban farms are also confronting questions about whether to participate in the high-priced, organic farmers' markets cropping up around the country.

"It's important to us that the food we grow here is available to people in the community," says the Food Project's Andrews. "That means it's not sold at the prices it would be if it was sold downtown." Selling at high-end markets is an issue that the Food Project grapples with because it has the potential to allow the organization to sustain itself. Right now, the group makes around $20,000 off the produce grown on its Dorchester land. If the Food Project sold it at the Copley Square farmers' market, opposite the Neiman Marcus, Andrews estimates they could get twice as much. "I think there is a sense at the organization that it could lend something to the urban agriculture movement if we were economically sustainable."

So far, however, the Food Project is opting out. "Our community is patient with what goes along with urban agriculture. Sometimes our compost smells, or we'll have a little rat infestation," Andrews says. "If we were selling downtown, it could become uncomfortable. I don't think it would make a whole lot of sense."

Because of funding difficulties, over the years many community food projects have died, which hurts those communities that have come to rely on their resources.

"Everyone keeps reinventing this thing over and over again, which tells me it has a really important function, and it should be supported," says Lawson. "But we shouldn't have to keep finding new land and new leaders."

For this reason, Lawson stresses land ownership as one path to sustainability. "The exact audience will change over time—but the hardest thing is transforming that space, that earth," she says. "Once you have that tillable soil, it's there for whatever programs want to come along and claim it. The gardeners need to look at land use and ownership of sites, and work with the city to keep them permanent." . . .

From Worthless to Valuable

For urban agriculturists it all comes back to empowering and investing in community. "[W]e expect to see more people of all ages and backgrounds first becoming educated food consumers, and then becoming engaged food citizens," concludes the Community Food Projects Competitive Grants Program 10 year progress report. "As healthful food and healthy eating become the norm, we anticipate that more people will look for broader regional and policy-based answers to the problems that continue to beset their communities."

But for Allen and her colleagues, food is not only an end, it's the means. "We're working towards a just world where everyone has full bellies and land and water," she says. "We're using food as a tool to get there. And it's completely doable."

| "Cuba [has] emerged as a leader in the
field of urban food production."

Cuba Provides a Model for Urban Agriculture

Alison Blay-Palmer

Alison Blay-Palmer is an associate professor at Wilfrid Laurier University in Ontario, Canada, where she teaches sustainable economics and alternative food systems. In the following viewpoint, Blay-Palmer examines the período especial in Cuba, when the fall of the Soviet Union deeply affected Cuba's food security and left the small island nation without the Soviet food imports it had relied on since the early 1960s. In response to its food crisis, Blay-Palmer explains, the Cuban government undertook a massive overhaul of its farming industry, engaging its rich social history as well as introducing concepts of sustainable agriculture to farmers who had previously focused almost entirely on growing sugar cane for export. According to Blay-Palmer, the Ministry of Agriculture quickly began to champion organic growing methods, especially in regard to the use of pesticides and herbicides. Unused land was redistributed to encourage as much local, urban farming as possible. Overall, argues the author, the Cuban food production system has been extremely successful, with the average Cuban meeting or exceeding standard daily nutritional requirements for

Alison Blay-Palmer, "Lessons from Cuba," *Land Research Action Network*, December 23, 2009. Copyright © 2009. All rights reserved. Reproduced by permission. See also FoodForeThought.

calories and protein. Despite obvious climate and political differ-
ences, Blay-Palmer says, Cuba's move from an industrial system of
food production to a largely organic, urban-based, local system can
serve as an example for other countries looking to maximize their
food production potential and end food insecurity to the greatest
degree possible.

As you read, consider the following questions:

1. What kind of composting is most often used in Cuban farming, according to the author?
2. According to Blay-Palmer, what kind of farm was most prevalent in Cuba prior to 1989? What kind was most prevalent after?
3. What kind of draft animal does the author state that Cuban farmers use most?

The impact of the *Período especial* [Special Period, the years of economic depression in Cuba brought on by the collapse of the Soviet Union in 1991] should not be underestimated. As a Cuban woman explained to me, the fall of the Soviet system was catastrophic. In her words it was as if, "We had built the house and all we had left to do was put the roof on. But then the rains came and washed all of our work away."

Between the late 1980s and 1993 in post-Soviet Cuba, nourishment plummeted from near-acceptable levels (based on FAO [UN Food and Agriculture Organisation] guidelines) of 2,400 kilocalories per person to about 1,860 kilocalories. Part of this shift was due to Cuba's reliance on food imports and the focus on sugar as its primary export crop. Prior to 1990, sugar accounted for more than 75% of all commodity exports while at the same time Cuba relied on imports of wheat (100%), beans (90–99%), oil and lard (68–94%), rice (50%) and milk and dairy products (38%) to feed its people. The combined reliance on Soviet imports and Soviet demand for Cuban product was compounded by a series of blockades and anti-Cuban policy emanating from the US that began in the early 1960s.

Facing the food security crisis of the early 1990s, Cuba moved aggressively to restore food access using a multi-pronged approach. By leveraging existing human resources and research infrastructure, redistributing land, introducing low-input sustainable agriculture, and taking preliminary steps towards market incentives, Cuba emerged as a leader in the field of urban food production. While of interest in itself, the Cuban story raises many flags for people debating the merits of food sovereignty and acceptable levels of regional food self-sufficiency.

Leveraging Human Resources

Thanks to a strong sense of community, social approval goes a long way in Cuba. Cuba has a vibrant musical tradition in part because of the support youth receive as they learn to play. Old-timers mentor up-and-coming musicians in clubs around Havana where their accomplishments are recognized and celebrated. Food is no different.

'Old' food processing techniques were gleaned from the older members of the community by [a] 17 year-old Havana entrepreneur. The teen set up a canning operation in his kitchen to preserve fruit, grow herbs in tires and other reclaimed containers, and offer courses to other people in Havana neighbourhoods. He targets youth through his work but shares his learning with all members of the community. He was recognized for his entrepreneurial and community-minded spirit with several awards and was held up as an example to visitors as one of the ways forward in urban food preservation and processing. In fact, he was the first stop during my visit. He was experimenting with different fruits and had cans of pineapple and mango as well as different preserves such as jams. He also dries herbs for teas and medicinal purposes. In this case, there was an emphasis on human and social capital as the food community was rebuilt around the preservation of food.

The role of incentives and social approval was very important on the farms I visited. The primary incentive program was a ranking system that classified urban farms based on their participation in a number of progressive projects. For example, one farm I visited was the first farm in Havana to experiment with aquaculture. As they also had a high diversity of crops and an irrigation system, this farm had the highest rating of all the farms I toured. Each farm group, whether a co-operative or a family run farm, was quick to point out and proud to display their level of achievement. This system encourages infrastructure as well as technological and crop diversity as a way to build resilience. In this context, social recognition was critical to achieving goals of food self-sufficiency.

Another facet of social ties is the strong links that are forged between urban farmers and their communities. First, farmers are required to be self-sufficient and produce for themselves. On one farm I visited this meant that the three-person (wife, husband and cousin) workforce ate off their small-holding. For larger co-operative farms, kitchens were in place on-site and everyone ate a noon meal together. On one farm I visited, over twenty people shared their midday meal in a common eating space. I took part in several of these meals as people generously shared their food. During my visit, I was treated to delicious soups, bean dishes and ham sandwiches. These meals are genuine 'slow food' experiences as farm workers break bread and socialize with one another. These meals help to build on-farm communities. The second farm obligation is to help feed their community as each farm is paired with a community organization—a hospital, a daycare, school or senior citizen residence. The farm must provide a set amount of produce to their community partner on a regular basis. In this way, urban-farmers are strongly embedded in their communities.

Introducing Sustainable Agriculture

Creating raised organic vegetable beds (known famously as 'organiponicos'), Cubans reformed degraded land and turned it into productive, enriched gardens. This allowed farmers to re-claim land. In some cases where buildings had collapsed—this was not uncommon as tens of buildings failed every year, the victims of insufficient funds to maintain them. In other cases, parking lots and brownfields [polluted industrial tracts] were the sites for urban farming. Frequently, building debris was used to contain soil.

Backed by the Ministry of Agriculture, the human resources mobilized to support the transition to sustainable urban agriculture were remarkable. In 1997 Havana had 67 extension agents, and 12 seed houses centred on TCAs (*Tiendas Consultario Agricola*, or agricultural consulting stores). The goal was to ramp this up to 50 stores and 500 professional extension agents and technicians. The advice and surveillance offered by technical experts about pest and weed management, along with input about seeds, soil improvers, and biological products meant that human know-how and diligence replaced chemicals. When I toured farms I was told that extension experts visited farms on a weekly, or, if needed, daily, basis to help inspect crops. This enabled early and targeted intervention in the case of disease or pests. This rapid, focused approach to support the conversion to urban agriculture represents a structural overhaul as the food system shifted from rural-based export market-dominated food production to urban food production for local consumption.

Technical innovation was key to maximizing the impact of increased human resources. A technical expert explained that Cuba was using many different biological approaches for pest and disease control including pheromone technologies. Direct and frequent links between farmers and government technicians created a more intensive agricultural system in urban areas designed to mitigate problems before they develop into crises. This also spreads knowledge as extension experts visit several farms so that improvements to systems such as vermi-composting spread from one area to another. . . . As of 2003, the Crop Protection Institute operated over 220 centers to provide inexpensive and ready access to beneficial insects and microorganisms for biological pest control in plants. There were even simpler, lower level interventions. For example, one farm had a garden for seedlings that was enclosed in cactus to prevent rabbits from eating the young plants.

Vermi-composting looms large in Cuban urban agriculture. Worms crank out tons of top quality compost every year. This rich ingredient is key to the productivity of urban farms. In 2001, Cuban farmers generated one million tons of natural compost. By 2003 they were producing fifteen million tons of organic matter. Compost is the basis for beginning gardens and remediating poor quality soil. On one farm I visited, they were experimenting with siphoning water from their compost and windrows to use as an intensive liquid fertilizer that could be applied in a concentrated form to give soil and plants a boost. This kind of ad hoc experimentation empowered farmers and seemed to be an important innovation, helping to improve resources for all farmers as ideas were disseminated through the network of technology specialists.

Rebuilding the Food System

As a result of the unique political dynamic, Cuba was able to activate huge land reform to facilitate the transition to urban agriculture. In an attempt to get state land into the hands of smaller-scale farmers and co-operatives, the Cuban government undertook a land devolution initiative. Between 1989 and 1997, this meant a shift in the type of farms. In 1989, state farms accounted for 80.7% by type. This fell to 48.7% by 1997 while the number of co-operatives increased from 8.6% to 39.4%. In addition to making more land available to grow food for domestic consumption, land resources were leveraged in a variety of ways.

In addition to social and technological innovation, Cuba also had to devise new ways of managing land. As a result several different land management arrangements emerged. 'Unidad Básica de Producción Cooperativa,' or the Basic Unit of Agricultural Production (UBPC) was the land reform that altered the farm landscape as the land for UBPCs was converted from former state farms. The UBPC uses a co-operative model so that all workers share in the productivity of the farm and benefit from the sale of crops. In the Havana context, the ability to effectively market crops depended very much on 'location . . . location . . . location'. Two farms I visited were located near relatively more affluent Havana communities—one was in the embassy district—and were able to grow and market higher value-added products. In one case, farm workers were earning more than four times the basic monthly allowance guaranteed to all Cubans. To put this in context, the additional income gave farm workers more disposable income than doctors. This was possible because once urban farmers fed themselves and met their community obligation any surplus could be sold through farmers' markets. In some cases these were formal market stands, in others, there were more informal connections with people in the community. The effect of these markets for Cuban citizens was increased access to fresh produce as they no longer depended on food shipped in from rural areas. Given the lack of fuel and parts for transportation vehicles, this empowered local communities and freed up resources for other uses. Another vehicle for change was the Patio Comunitario (community gardens). . . . The Patio Comunitario initiative was developed to increase food security for the most vulnerable Cubans at the micro scale. The goal for community gardens was to have a production capacity garden for every fifteen houses. As part of this initiative, backyards, parks and verges were dedicated to food production. And no land was considered out of bounds. If someone wanted to cultivate a lot an occupant was not using for food, the person could apply to get access to the land. I was told that usually within six months a decision would be made about using the piece of land for growing food.

The Achievements and Challenges

Many gains have been made thanks to the Cuban drive to use urban agriculture to address food sovereignty challenges. The numbers back up the move to a more robust food system. Comparing 1989 to 2003, the Ministry of Agriculture reported the renewed use of animal traction power so that there were 2,400 teams of oxen labor in the City of Havana. There were also huge decreases in the amount of inputs as Cuba was using half the diesel fuel, ten percent of the chemical fertilizers and seven percent of the synthetic insecticides by 2003 when compared to 1997 levels. By 2000, the daily food per capita had risen to 2,600 calories per day, exceeding FAO recommended levels of 2,400 calories. Remarkably, they were also meeting almost 95% of their daily protein requirements. By 2003, urban agriculture employed over 20,000 Cubans. It accounted for 22% of job growth between 2002 and 2003. To put the scale of the Cuban achievement in context, in 1997 it was estimated that urban agriculture produced 0.1 million tons of produce. By the middle of 2003, the country was on track to achieve 3.4 million tons of produce for the year.

Despite some remaining challenges, the acute food shortage crisis is essentially over. As a result, Cuba provides a leading example of large-scale success in moving a food system away from industrial style agriculture to urban based, local food production. While under considerable duress, Cuba made heroic efforts to construct its own version of a food secure space for its citizens, and has in some ways shown the way for other countries as they aspire to use urban agriculture. Of course, some problem areas remain, especially regarding milk, meat, and eggs, which continue to require imported animal feed that strain limited resources. Rice, usually grown on large state farms, has also consistently fallen short of planned levels of production. For example in 2003, Cuba was able to meet only 57% of its domestic rice requirements. Even in these areas, there is hope for the future.

A very encouraging technological development is the introduction of a new approach to growing rice called the System of Rice Intensification (SRI) known as SICA (*Sistema Intensivo de Cultivo Arrocero*) in Cuba. This new approach is promoted world-wide by, among others, the Cornell International Institute for Food, Agriculture and Development. In Cuba, this technology has been pioneered and tested by Dr. Rena Perez, Luis Romero and the Cuban Rice Research Institute. In field tests root numbers increased over 8 times and yields increased up to fourfold while seed, water, and petroleum requirements are reduced. Optimistic rice experts are claiming that Cuba is potentially on its way to self-sufficiency in rice.

Some Qualifications

While Cuba provides an exciting example of the potential for new food systems it is important to make some qualifications before discussing its relevance to other contexts. First, the climate of Cuba must be considered. Cuba has a year-long growing season in terms of heat and daylight given its mid-latitude location. This semi-tropical to temperate climate allows for year-round food production. For example, potatoes are seeded in September for an April harvest. Second, there are unique political circumstances to contemplate. The transition to a stable post–Fidel Castro situation is well under way. However, there are substantial US interests who see Cuba as a potential branch-plant opportunity for food products such as citrus. As a 1998 *Tampa Tribune* article observed, "Before Fidel Castro rose to power in 1959, Cuba supplied the United States with a third of its winter vegetables, 3 million tons of sugar a year, and enjoyed close ties to Florida agricultural buyers. Cuba has several advantages, [a University of Florida economist] said. The island has an abundance of fertile farmland and faces no threat of a crop-destroying freeze, plus Cuban farmers do not have to contend with the expensive environmental safeguards in place in the U.S. and other countries." While this does not necessarily represent current mainstream thinking in the US, it is an attitude that may have to be considered as new political realities play themselves out. Finally, the ability of the central government under Castro to rapidly realign land and human resources during the Special Period is not transferable to other countries.

So, while acknowledging these exceptional circumstances, there are take away lessons for other countries aspiring to integrate more urban agriculture into their food systems. First, there is huge value in empowering people and allowing them access to land to be more self-sufficient. Given current debates about the merits of re-localizing food systems, the power of putting land into the hands of people is important to consider. Second, there may be merits in connecting urban agriculture projects to community groups as a way to build social cohesion. Third, Cuban urban agriculture underlines the merits of low technology approaches to affordable, healthy, abundant food production. This is good news as the capital costs are relatively low while the benefits could be substantial. The Cuban experiment inspires others around the world to move in more sustainable urban food production directions. Meanwhile, within Cuba the more open-market experiment provides rich ground for Cuba to build on strong foundations of community participation and sustainable urban agriculture.

| "Cuban urban agriculture, no matter how inspiring, is largely irrelevant to Americans."

Cuba's Urban Agriculture Model Is Irrelevant for Americans

Andy Fisher

Andy Fisher is co-founder and director of the Oregon-based Community Food Security Coalition and a fellow with the Institute for Agriculture and Trade Policy. In the following viewpoint, Fisher argues that, while Cuba's post-Soviet period of agricultural revolution is impressive and inspiring, it is irrelevant to the discussion of urban agriculture in Western democracies because of its dependence on strong state involvement in land distribution—as of 2008 anyone in Cuba can request the use of vacant land and receive an informal title to that parcel for as long as forty years—and state control of salaries so that the pay of farm workers is high compared even with that of professionals. Additionally, says Fisher, technical subsidies and land distribution programs allow urban farmers to operate with very little overhead, and the country's state-controlled market ensures little competition from other sources. Contrasted with Cuba, Fisher asserts, farming in the United States is an open enterprise dependent largely upon market competition and the farmer's ability to pay rent or make mortgage payments on the land as well as machinery, workers, and general overhead.

As you read, consider the following questions:
1. How does Fisher describe the differences between the US and Cuban economies?
2. How does Cuba's approach to public land distribution differ from land tenure in the United States, in the author's opinion?
3. Ultimately, how did Cuba change its manufacturing economy as a result of the "special period" according to Fisher?

Among the adherents of the food security movement in the United States, many idolize Cuba's experience in building a vibrant urban farming sector. This idealization is due to the lack of information available on the Cuban system, as caused by the travel embargo and media blackout there. Compounding this situation is the vast difference between the Cuban and American political and economic systems.

Cuba's accomplishments are undeniably astounding, inspiring and a testament to the country's flexibility and pragmatism: 350,000 new well paying jobs (out of a total workforce of 5 million) created in urban agriculture nationally; 4 million tons of fruits and vegetables produced annually in Havana, up ten-fold in a decade; and a city of 2.2 million people regionally self-sufficient in produce. These accomplishments have been supported by an extensive network of input suppliers, technical assistance providers, researchers, teachers and government agencies.

Yet, Cuban urban agriculture, no matter how inspiring, is largely irrelevant to Americans. The state is pervasive throughout Cuba and controls virtually all aspects of the official economy. The government can mobilize quickly and massively around its priorities through an array of powerful policy tools at its disposal. After 50 years of socialist rule, Cuban institutions, as well as the mentality and expectations of the Cuban public, differ vastly from those in the U.S. By way of example, the ruling motto of Cuban urban agriculture states, "We must decentralize only up to a point where control is not lost, and centralize only up to a point where initiative is not killed" embodies the vast differences between their planned economy and our free market system.

The fundamental differences between the Cuban and American systems as they relate to the success of urban agriculture are vast and, for the most part, are insurmountable.

Land Ownership Is Key

Case in point, the success of urban agriculture in Cuba has been grounded in the distribution of public land for food production. For example, a law passed in 2008 allowed any citizen or entity to request idle lands up to 33 acres to be passed out in usufruct [for practical use] for 20–40 years. This law resulted in 16,000 persons requesting land in the past two years. Since all land in Cuba—with the exception of private homes—is the property of the State, the government has resources at its disposal to support its policies far beyond that of any American jurisdiction.

On the other hand, in the U.S., land use laws and private property land tenure represent a very real challenge to the expansion of urban farming. While some cities have made their minimal idle lands available for urban farming, when they do so, garden land tenure is not assured. For example, in New York City, hundreds of community gardens were threatened with destruction and dozens were ultimately plowed under when city government prioritized housing developments.

Land use planners here typically view urban agriculture as an interim land use at best, until a development opportunity with higher economic utility, such as housing, retail or manufacturing, becomes feasible. Few communities have protected urban agriculture as a permanent use in their planning documents, although this phenomenon is beginning to change.

Neighbor complaints about noises, smells, visual clutter and dust created by urban farming are made frequently and deter farm permanence.

Salary Controls Abet Cuban Farming

In Cuba, virtually everyone works for the State. The State sets salaries; economic incentives are controlled by the government. To incentivize fruit and vegetable production, the government has allowed urban agricultural enterprises to distribute part of their profits back to the workers. These quasi-free enterprise farming operations have led to some unique salary structures wherein farm workers can earn two or three times the salary of the local physicians. These incentives have thus allowed urban farms to retain high quality human resources and maximize production.

U.S. policymakers have few tools at their disposal to shape the earnings of urban agricultural producers, beyond the nigh-impossible extension of commodity subsidies. Urban farms have to compete with the rest of the labor market for qualified workers, with immigration policy also playing a large factor in agricultural labor supply.

Profit, Capital, and the Marketplace

The economic conditions under which Cuban urban farms operate are extraordinarily different than the conditions of similar enterprises in the U.S. For example, since they do not purchase or rent the land, they have no mortgage or rental costs to pay. Inputs and technical assistance are subsidized by the government. (A visit from a technician to assess a pest problem costs one cooperative member the equivalent of two bits [twenty-five cents].) They enjoy little competition from other sources for their fruits and vegetables, which they may sell at farmers' markets or at on-site farm stands. While capital may be difficult to access from the government, there is no private banking sector and no interest charges to bear. As a result, the urban farms in Havana are profitable enough to redistribute a significant portion of their earnings (85 percent in one case) back to the workers. In a country where the basic wage is $10 per month and a monthly incentive of $50 per month is quite substantial, these farms clearly do not need to be making enormous profits to make a difference in the lives of their workers.

Running a profitable urban farming business in the U.S. entails a much more complex set of calculations than in Cuba. In the U.S., small farms struggle to break even, under the weight of high monthly payments for land, inputs and machinery. On the wholesale level, they face difficult access to markets for selling their products and typically receive prices near or below their cost of production. Small farms selling directly to consumers frequently face stiff competition from other farmers or other retail outlets, which are typically better capitalized. The more socially-minded farming enterprises subsidize their operations with grants for educational programs or through agri-tourism schemes. To be profitable, urban farmers must find a market niche at which they excel, such as providing ultra-fresh micro-greens to high-end restaurants or through cause-related marketing.

Necessity Is the Mother of Invention

Cuba's shift to urban and organic agriculture was driven by necessity. As the Soviet bloc fell in the late 1980s and early 1990s, Cuba lost the primary market for its products and its source of subsidized agricultural inputs and petroleum. The crisis that ensued was referred to by the Orwellian [reminiscent of dystopian novelist George Orwell] term, "the special period," and they were hungry and dark times for Cuba. To its credit, the Cuban government found partial solutions to this emergency by pushing the country toward organic and urban agriculture. As one highly placed Cuban official said about the decision to support urban farming and farmers' markets, "We moved food production and the markets as close to the people as possible because there was no oil for transportation to get the people out to the food." This policy decision came at an ideological cost. It entailed a partial

71

opening of urban food production to the free market, which resulted in increased social inequality through income distortions. It also was a 180-degree turn from the capital and input-intensive, Soviet-influenced production methods valued in Cuba at the time.

American interest in urban agriculture has been influenced by the state of the economy. Backyard vegetable production and seed sales for 2009 spiked significantly over 2008 levels, and urban farming in Detroit has grown rapidly as a means to deal with acres of vacant land. But, by and large, increased policymaker and public interest in urban agriculture is traced to concerns about food literacy, urban sustainability, community building, obesity prevention and—to a lesser degree—economic development and job training. These goals are important, but they are not driven by a state of emergency as Cuba suffered.

The success of Cuba's urban agriculture program is a true inspiration to the people working to green cities here in the U.S. Yet, what is best learned from Cuba's experience is not the specifics of how to produce more food in urban communities, but the value of alternative economic, political and social structures that can help us accomplish our goals.

Periodical and Internet Sources Bibliography

The following articles have been selected to supplement the diverse views presented in this chapter.

David Adam	"Food Price Rises Threaten Global Security—UN," *Guardian* (Manchester, UK), April 9, 2008.
Nick Amies	"Land Grabs, Biofuel Demand Raise Global Food-Security Risk," Deutsche Welle, July 15, 2011. www.dw-world.de.
Lael Brainard	"A Food Security Strategy We Can't Afford Not to Fund," *Guardian* (Manchester, UK), June 16, 2011.
Lester Brown	"The World Is Only One Poor Harvest Away from Chaos," *Grist*, January 12, 2011.
Tracy Hampton	"Food Insecurity Harms Health, Well-Being of Millions in the United States," *Journal of the American Medical Association*, October 24–31, 2007.
Claudia Kalb	"Food Insecurity Rising in America," *Newsweek*, August 10, 2010.
Joanna Lin	"'Food Insecurity' Reaches Record High," California Watch, November 16, 2010. www.californiawatch.org.
Peter Mandelson	"Food Insecurity," *New York Times*, May 22, 2008.
Danielle Nierenberg	"Targeting Gaps in the Food Supply Chain: Going Beyond Agricultural Production to Achieve Food Security," Salem-News.com, July 14, 2011. www.salem-news.com.
Paul Teng, Margarita Escaler, and Mely Caballero-Anthony	"Urban Food Security: Feeding Tomorrow's Cities," *Significance Magazine*, June 2011.

CHAPTER 2

Is Urban Agriculture Economically Sustainable?

Chapter Preface

In December 2007 violence broke out in the East African country of Kenya following the announcement of election results. With incumbent president Mwai Kibaki declared the winner, supporters of his opponent, Raila Odinga, accused Kibaki of manipulating election results. And because the two candidates came from rival ethnic tribes, the violence soon became ethnically driven and lasted for months. Some of the most extreme rioting took place in Kibera, the largest slum in Kenya and one of the largest in all of Africa, located in the Kenyan capital of Nairobi. Estimates vary greatly as to the number of residents of Kibera, ranging from an official government tally of 170,000 to more realistic counts of up to a million or more people living in an area of just over one-and-a-half square miles. The settlement has existed in one form or another since the end of World War I, when plots of land were provided by the British colonial government to members of the Nubian tribe who had served in the war, but the Kenyan government provides no services to the slum and does not acknowledge it as a legal settlement.

Yet despite the absence of running water, electricity, and sanitation services, and in the midst of persistent rioting during which no food from rural regions was allowed to enter the slum for a month, a group of mostly women farmers in Kibera took matters into their own hands. Although they have no land tenure—the land of Kibera is all owned by the National Social Security Fund—people in Kibera, most of whom have migrated from the rural parts of Kenya in search of jobs in Nairobi, have operated small-scale urban farms on tiny plots throughout the slum neighborhood for decades. When the French nongovernmental organization Solidarités International offered women farmers training and supplies, the women found a new way to grow food for themselves and their neighbors, in large recycled bags or sacks, called "vertical gardens."

Filled with soil and stones, the sacks function as small portable gardens. Small plots of land in the slum are set aside to start the seeds, which are transplanted into the sacks when they are large enough. Each sack can hold multiple plants because holes are punched vertically into the sides, with a seedling planted in each hole. Erick Wamanja, writing in the online *Kibera Journal* in July 2010, noted that a single sack "can hold 50 seedlings of kales or spinach and 20 tomato plants." According to a 2009 press release on the program from Solidarités International, participating households have not only increased their own food security but in many cases have grown enough surplus food to sell either to their neighbors in Kibera or at markets in Nairobi, earning them an estimated thirty-three (US) dollars extra per month—more than the average monthly income in Kibera. Wamanja quoted a Kibera gardener and community mobilizer trained by Solidarités International: "Asha Zaidi . . . says the project has reached all the eight villages in Kibera and women are busier than ever before working on their gardens. Ms. Zaidi, who teaches residents how to prepare the gardens, says they have trained and given out seedlings to about 3,000 people in each village and the demand is growing." Although these people have no alternative, the urban farmers in other cities in the world are usually not so desperate and often pursue their gardening and farming as an additional source of income. The authors of the viewpoints in the following chapter debate the sustainability of urban agriculture.

"*[Urban agriculture] provides some answers to the unique social, economic and environmental challenges posed by fast urban growth.*"

The Economic Success of Urban Agriculture Depends on the Farming Method

Paule Moustier and George Danso

Paule Moustier is a food marketing researcher for the French organization CIRAD Agricultural Research for Development. George Danso has a PhD in agricultural and resource economics from the University of Alberta, Canada. In the following viewpoint, the authors examine the challenges posed by rapid urban growth in terms of the ability to provide ample employment, economic development, and food sources for inhabitants. In general, the authors maintain that urban agriculture can be a solution to this massive influx of people from rural to urban areas, but the economic results both for individual farmers and for the larger economy and overall standard of living depend upon the kind of farming operation that is undertaken. Subsistence farmers, for example, are those whose families are so poor that they must consume all of their farming output, and the work is typically seasonal. Small family commercial farmers, on the other hand, usually earn enough from their farms to break even financially, although a large portion must work at second jobs. Large-scale urban agricultural entrepreneurs tend to be invested mostly in livestock, fish farms, or produce, and they are able to hire salaried workers. Nonetheless, there is a high rate of failure of these ventures. Overall, however, the authors find that urban farming can make a difference to a city's economy—depending on which kind of farming is done and whether or not the urban farmers are able to move from one type of farming to another.

As you read, consider the following questions:

1. How do the authors differentiate between family-type commercial farmers and agricultural entrepreneurs?
2. Why do Moustier and Danso suggest that urban land in some cities would be better left for housing and development rather than agriculture?
3. What do the authors state are the issues that concern different types of farmers moving from one type of farming to another?

If urban agriculture [UA] is attracting the growing attention of researchers, policy makers and diverse development stakeholders, it is mostly because it provides some answers to the unique social, economic and environmental challenges posed by fast urban growth. The dramatic speed of urban growth in developing countries has not been paralleled with the development of enterprises and infrastructure needed to absorb the new employment needs, by contrast to the developed countries where urban development has been much slower. Finally, the context of fast liberalisation and restrictions in the public sector has reduced the possibilities of employment in public administration, traditionally a major provider of employment in cities.

Yet, peri-urban agriculture is still a subject of debate as regards its viability and the necessity for it to receive political support. In a challenging paper, [Frank] Ellis and [James] Sumberg provide a number of reasons why scarce public resources should not target urban agriculture. The report stresses that in the light of high land costs in urban areas and the fact that there is still not enough land to cater [to] housing and infrastructure needs, it would seem legitimate to let agriculture move towards rural areas whilst improving the transport infrastructure at the same time, as has been the case in Europe. Moreover, urban agriculture is subjected to many types of pollution and is itself a pollutant. In fact, urban agriculture takes advantage of market distortions and can be only transient. But most to the point, the authors looked at the lack of rigorous quantitative data to assess the social, economic and environmental impact of urban agriculture, and compare it with alternative sources of incomes in the city, alternative uses of land, and alternative sources of food.

In her analysis of the case studies prepared for the ETC reader on urban agriculture in 2000 [titled *Growing Cities, Growing Food*], Rachel Nugent also points out the informal, small-scale character of UA, and its little impact in terms of income injection into the economy: "Agriculture is a residual activity within imperfect markets. As such, it is conducted opportunistically and with relatively little investment. Farmers are more induced in self-subsistence rather than looking at income opportunities". The survival strategies of urban farmers has also been brought to the fore by [Michael] Lipton as part of his famous "urban bias" theory in which he describes urban producers as "fringe villagers, waiting until penury forces them back to the land and meanwhile living on casual work or on their rural relatives". In fact, UA is often presented with the characteristics found typical of the informal sector, which have been summarised by [Williamson E.] Cole and [Bichaka] Fayissa as small size, family management, labour intensiveness and extra-legal nature. These characteristics generate what economists call the simple reproduction of the enterprise, i.e. the impossibility to generate more than the income necessary for the enterprise to pay for the inputs and means of production involved, and hence the impossibility for the enterprise to accumulate savings and invest in its development. This process has been particularly well described by a series of studies on UA in Zambia: poor gardeners are caught up in a vicious circle when they plant a garden because their jobs do not provide them with enough cash income to feed their family, and they cannot grow more food and thus save money because they do not have cash to buy agricultural inputs, e.g., manure, wastes or fertilisers—a typical poverty trap.

Yet empirical data on urban agriculture generated in the last ten years helps analysts to go beyond the image of the subsistence farmer as the dominant type in urban agriculture. The number of case studies on urban and peri-urban agriculture has increased rapidly and are a comprehensive and valuable source in evaluating the economic and market role and comparative advantage of farming in and around cities. The methods, both in terms of conceptual frameworks and data collection, have improved to take better account of the specific features of urban agriculture, especially its numerous non-market costs and benefits, as well as its non-market organisational features based on the logic of location and risk alleviation, for which economics of proximity, combining insights from spatial and institutional economics, provide relevant analytical tools. While a frequent focus of prior studies has been the opposition between the informal urban agricultural sector and the urban environment, particularly in terms of policy, the benefits of alliances between agriculture and the urban environment are given more attention now, and a more balanced appreciation of the conflicts and synergies is looked for. It is only through such alliances that urban agriculture can break out of the transient remains of rural agriculture and really gain an "urban nature" as expressed by P. Donadieu and A. Fleury [in a 1997 article in the French journal *Annals of Urban Research*].

Diversity Strategies

According to UNDP [United Nations Development Program], 80 percent of families in Libreville (Congo), 68 percent of urban dwellers in six Tanzanian cities, 45 percent in Lusaka (Zambia), 37 percent in Maputo (Mozambique), 36 percent in Ouagadougou (Burkina Faso), [and] 35 percent in Yaoundé (Cameroon) are involved in urban agriculture. The involvement of so many people in urban agriculture indicates its centrality amongst informal-sector activities. Yet the reasons for getting involved in urban agriculture, and consequently, its social and economic impact, vary across different categories of households. A major feature of UA is indeed the diversity of the socio-economic profiles of actors involved, and their varying income and livelihood strategies. Thus, the valuation of socio-economic impact will be different according to the types that are referred to, and not taking this into consideration may lead to differing estimates. Several attempts to classify urban agricultural systems have been made which can be summarised into the types below. . . .

Subsistence Home (Intra-) Urban Farmers

This category involves urban residents who farm around their homes or elsewhere near the city, mostly for subsistence purposes. They raise staple food crops, vegetables, small livestock, and sometimes trees. [P.] Drechsel et al. documents that every second household is engaged in some form of subsistence production in Accra, Ghana. The production is typically seasonal, and the output is used mainly for home consumption, in addition to market purchases. There may also be the occasional sale of the surplus in the market. These survival strategies have been documented by a number of case studies including the ones reviewed by Nugent. Typical examples are maize growing in the districts of Yaoundé, Accra metropolis and Harare [Zimbabwe]; rice growing in Tamale, Ghana and Bandim, Bissau; and multi-cropped fields cultivated seasonally by elderly women in Brazzaville

[Congo] on the outskirts of the city. Food from subsistence type production is usually of better quality, lower in cost and is more consistently accessible than purchased food.

Family-Type Commercial Farmers

Family-type commercial farmers appear to be the dominant type in terms of importance in urban food supply, if not in terms of numbers. The typical crops grown are vegetables. What these farmers have in common is a family background in agriculture, which may also be in relation to ethnicity. For instance in Buenos Aires [Argentina] where the vegetable growers are mostly Bolivian, the Japanese [there] mostly grow herbs and the Italians grow trees. Another common feature of these farmers is that they have searched for alternative employment having experienced failures in their studies or former employment; this also reflects the difficult employment situation in African cities, especially for poorly qualified people. Three-fourths of the interviewed vegetable growers in Brazzaville mentioned failures in other jobs as mechanics, taxi drivers, cooks etc. before getting into agriculture. Urban agriculture thus enables the employment of urban people who are quite vulnerable from an economic point of view—yet not as vulnerable as the subsistence farmers. But the activity seldom generates enough income for savings and investment, all the more since access to land is insecure.

In contrast with subsistence urban farmers, who mainly produce for self-consumption, commercial urban and peri-urban farmers are involved in agriculture to earn a monetary income to pay for the numerous expenses in an urban environment (housing, children's schooling, medical expenses). Although they may consume some of their produce, it is only a small portion. Agriculture represents their main household source of income, which may be in addition to other sources of income. In Yaoundé, more than 70 percent of intra-urban farmers do not have other occupations; this figure is 85 percent in Abidjan [Côte d'Ivoire]. In Yaoundé, again, 70 percent of commercial producers cited agriculture as their principal source of income, 21 percent cited a job in the formal sector and the remaining 9 percent cited petty commerce. By contrast to these figures, 67 percent of household food producers cited a formal sector job as their principal source of income, 20 percent cited petty commerce, and the remaining 13 percent cited their pension. While none cited agriculture as their principal income source, approximately half did say it was their second most important source of revenue.

In peri-urban Hanoi [Vietnam], alongside commerce and craft work, agriculture still provider more than half of the incomes in a municipality such as Trung Trac. Forty four of 100 farmers surveyed in Cagayan de Ore, Philippines, indicated vegetable production as their main source of livelihood.

As the farmers' objectives are to get regular food and income and secure their livelihoods, the cropping system has to be risk averse, yet have high value crops to cope with small size of land. This is typically the case of leafy vegetables, which are hardly sensitive to water excesses or shortages and to diseases. Their short cycles (two to three weeks) enable regular cash generation. The proportion of leafy vegetables in the cultivated area is 70 percent in Brazzaville. In Yaoundé, the focus on traditional leafy vegetables and green maize production is observed among both commercial producers and household food producers.

Production systems of this category display common characteristics: irrigation, use of organic matter, cultivation on beds, and small farm size (less than 1ha [hectare]). This reflects the necessary intensification per unit of land in a context of high pressure on land. As the farmers have differentiated access to land and capital (the higher the capital, the higher the presence of men in the business), the production systems display variations in the following aspects: the nature of crops grown (low-risk and short cycle crops, e.g. leafy vegetables, versus more risky and longer cycle crops, e.g. temperate vegetables or ornamental crops); the nature of agricultural inputs; equipment; marketing strategies. The intensification strategies of vegetable farmers have been especially well documented in Kumasi, Ghana by Danso et al. Depending on the availability of land, type of production system and location of the farm, the labour requirement differs. In the urban areas, where plot sizes are small, domestic labour is enough to cultivate the land area. In most peri-urban areas, hired, permanent and domestic labour is employed, depending on the above mentioned factors. As the main objective is to get a continuous income, the farmers may change plots and type of crops according to the time of the year. This may give an appearance of seasonality and discontinuity in the farmers' business, but in fact the activity usually continues, although at various locations. While in the dry season, vegetables are grown along the rivers and polluted streams, and with water from dugout wells, shallow groundwater and pipe borne water, farmers may move to non-flooded areas during the rainy season. This was observed in Brazzaville and Bangui [Central African Republic] where farmers have access to sloping land enabling them to move to higher ground to cope with flooding. In Bissau [Guinea-Bissau], on the other hand, women farmers had access only to plots located along the river (the non flooded plots were cultivated by civil servants) and they had to stop growing-vegetables in the rainy season, which also explained their limited income.

Urban Agricultural Entrepreneurs

The main differences between this category and the family commercial farmers are the scale of the farms and the use of salaried labour. Urban entrepreneurs, usually civil servants, businessmen or expatriates, invest in intensive temperate vegetable production, poultry keeping, fish farms, or fruit growing, often in combination or with income form other sources. They invest in infrastructure such as motor pumps, treadle pumps, shelters, buildings, and attempt at mechanising certain agricultural operations, e.g. irrigation or land tillage. They rely on a salaried labour force for doing most of the tasks. They may lack an agricultural background and the cases of losses and failures are numerous. They often control the marketing of their produce, e.g. through direct delivery to stores or with links to export companies. Some examples of this category are the producers of green beans around Dakar [Senegal], the civil servants involved in fruit production around Yaoundé, the chicken farmers around Ouagadougou and the poultry producers in and around Kumasi. In peri-urban Hanoi, the possibility of access to capital leads to land accumulation and other, non-agricultural, activities. This additional income is invested in agricultural diversification (moving away from rice cultivation to fish-farming, arboriculture [tree-growing] etc.) or commerce.

Multi-Cropping Peri-Urban Farmers

This category refers to farmers who share many of the characteristics of rural farmers (and may be called "rurban" farmers), except for the influence of the city in terms of production outlets with a growing share of marketed output; sources of incomes, including agricultural and non agricultural; level of intensification; and specialisation (e.g., having some vegetable fields). They are hardly threatened by urbanisation in terms of land pressure. This category has been extensively studied in Cameroon. The study reveals that agriculture is often only one of diverse options to generate food and income.

An important question of course is whether an urban farmer develops from one category to another? Is it possible for a farmer to evolve from being a subsistence type to a more commercial type, generate sufficient income and savings to increase the scale of business, and even move on to being an entrepreneurial type? The observation that most entrepreneurs originate from sectors other than agriculture suggests that commercial family farmers find it difficult to increase their scale of enterprise, and that they reach little more than to maintain (reproduce) their livelihood. This is due to a trap in terms of farm size and available capital, common to many enterprises of the informal sector, viewed as refuge options rather than paths for development. Yet there are some examples suggesting possible avenues for dynamic accumulation and growth from UA. Vegetable farmers in Lomé [Togo] and Cotonou [Benin] have moved from subsistence to commercial vegetable production, as their savings enabled them to use treadle pumps and then motor pumps, and most of them are now producing for export and local consumption. In Kenya, contractual farming agreements with livestock agro-industries has enabled farmers to generate substantial incomes. The initial conditions for farmers to enter into such a contract are space (being able to accommodate 300 chicks), the ability to pay for the costs for water, electricity, labour and basic equipment, and the payment of a deposit of US$ 0,8 per chick. A supporting system in terms of municipal legislation, technical skill development and credit provision is crucial for these patterns of accumulation.

Interestingly, although they are often documented as a necessary condition for farmers to gain easier access to resources, markets and investment, farmers' organisations are rarely documented as successful in paving the way for economic development.

| "*[Urban agriculture] presents entrepreneurial opportunities that could yield numerous living-wage green jobs.*"

Successful Entrepreneurial Urban Farming Requires Financial Investment

Green for All

Green for All is a US organization dedicated to building a green economy. In the following viewpoint, the authors consider the start-up costs of urban farming as a for-profit business to be steep but not prohibitive for many city residents, citing Small Business Administration loans, grants, and nonprofit monies as possible forms of financial support. The total initial investment, according to the authors, would be around ten thousand dollars for a farm of at least a half an acre within city limits. The authors suggest that a small urban farmer could also take advantage of a community-supported agriculture (CSA) program, farmers' markets, and farm stands to turn a profit in the first year of business. As examples, the authors study three urban farms—one in Newark, New Jersey, one in San Francisco, California, and a third in Portland, Oregon. The authors assert that each of these took a different approach to urban farming, and each has seen notable success.

As you read, consider the following questions:

1. According to the authors, what are some of the global issues that urban agriculture can address?
2. What are two potential problems for urban farmers cited by Green for All?
3. How does the viewpoint describe San Francisco's My Farm, and how its founder keeps it "greener than most"?

It is becoming increasingly difficult to find fresh, locally grown produce in America's cities. This is especially true in poorer urban neighborhoods. Many urban residents can find only food shipped in from thousands of miles away. Customers pay a price, as the cost of that shipping makes the food more expensive. And the environment pays a price, as shipping food by trucks, boats and planes is a major source of greenhouse gas pollution.

Urban agriculture seeks to avoid these oft-overlooked costs of shipping food by cultivating, processing, and distributing food within city limits. This increases the total supply of food available to a city, heightening its overall food security. Freshly grown on small plots of land, city-grown produce is also higher quality, increasing nutrition and reducing conditions resulting from bad eating habits, like obesity. Lastly, urban agriculture expands the economic base of a city through the production, processing, packaging, and marketing of consumable products. As such, it presents entrepreneurial opportunities that could yield numerous living-wage green jobs.

Why Is Urban Agriculture Important?

Urban farming can help us solve some of the key problems in our modern cities—global warming, rampant population growth, international food scares, domestic weight problems, the current economic malaise. But the practice predates all of those problems. Urban agriculture was common in ancient Persia, and helped sustain the Inca civilization in Machu Picchu. Even the

United States has experimented with widespread urban agriculture. During World Wars I and II, the government urged those not living in rural areas to plant food in their yards to relieve pressure on traditional agriculture to produce all the food necessary to support the war efforts. These "victory gardens" were successful too, growing roughly 40% of the vegetables consumed in the U.S. in 1942 and 1943.

That the "victory garden" effort was so successful is hardly surprising, given how simple and accessible urban farming can be. Urban farms can be located on plots of land as small as 4' × 8' in climates of all types, and even on concrete rooftops. One need not have a background in conventional farming or an advanced education to engage in urban agriculture. It is an industry open to all socioeconomic backgrounds. Dozens of different fruits (apples, cherries, and all types of berries) and vegetables (from arugula to zucchini) can be raised in myriad environments. Finally, the startup costs are surprisingly low, whereas the earnings potential can be quite lucrative. The result is a historically proven, sustainable industry that improves public health and provides its practitioners with a decent living wage.

Urban Farming as a Business

Urban farms come in a variety of shapes and sizes. Almost all, however, share some basic startup costs. Assuming a plot of land of at least half an acre, a list of such costs would likely include:

- Rototiller ($4,500): a motorized plow that uses rotating tines or blades to cultivate the soil and get the land ready for planting. This is the only mechanized equipment necessary.
- Coolers ($4,000): Two upright produce coolers used to store fresh vegetables and prevent spoilage.
- Other equipment ($1,000): garden seeder, wheel hoe, standard-issue tools, harvesting bins, hoses, and sprinklers
- Sales & Marketing ($500): farmers market tables, display

baskets, digital scale, signage
• TOTAL: $10,000

Admittedly, the aspiring urban farmer faces a number of obstacles in starting up her business. First, $10,000 is not a trivial sum of money to someone living in an underserved community, especially since such enterprises are usually self-financed. In addition, these startup costs do not include operating expenses for things such as seeds, bags, transportation, and farmers market fees. These expenses would depend greatly on sales goals, as well as any labor costs. They would likely come to anywhere between $5,000 and $10,000 per year for a typical sub-acre farm seeking $60,000 in gross revenue. Aside from startup and operating costs, there is the question of land. Few people living in a densely populated city have immediate access to a half-acre of tillable land. And even if one has the land ready, prohibitive zoning and land use regulations will occasionally hinder urban farmers.

Still, these hurdles are not insurmountable.

First, with regards to the startup costs, urban farms already attract a modest share of grants, Small Business Administration loans, and nonprofit support. Hopefully, not only will that continue, but lenders like the Farm Credit Council will begin extending loans to urban farms, too. Right now, such lenders support only rural farms, which already enjoy significant and increasing subsidies. Urban farms can also offset startup costs, as well as operating expenses, by initiating a community-supported agriculture (CSA) program, where customers purchase up-front memberships in exchange for regular allotments of produce later during the season. Other revenue opportunities include farmers markets, wholesale markets (restaurants, caterers, etc.), and possibly an on-site farm stand. These four market segments should help a first-year urban farm bring in anywhere from $10,000–$20,000—enough to potentially turn a small profit in the first year. As that farm develops its agricultural expertise, not to mention its sales channels, it can gross more than $60,000 with just a half acre of land.

Many cities have taken steps to make it easier for urban farmers to find usable land. Detroit, Cleveland, Brooklyn, Chicago, Pittsburgh, Philadelphia, and Newark (to name just a few) have struck land deals and, in some cases, relaxed their zoning restrictions.

One final fact also makes it easier for urban farmers to find usable real estate: land need not even be tillable to support urban agriculture. Farms have found success in the harshest of "urban jungles" using special containers packed with treated soil that serve as a suitable replacement to unspoilt land. (This would obviate the need for the rototiller above, but come at an incremental expense of roughly $10,000 for a half-acre farm, bringing startup costs closer to $15,000.) In this model, a farmer would plant vegetables in these containers and cultivate them much as if they were planted directly in the ground. Of course, one still needs access to land, even if it is covered with concrete. But as the case studies below make plain, urban agriculture is garnering a lot of support among many constituencies—a fact that might help ease the burden associated with finding available land.

Brick City Urban Farms

A collaboration among three entrepreneurs—John Taylor, Kirsten Giardi, and Lorraine Gibbons—Brick City is located in a fenced-in, half-acre property in downtown Newark, NJ. The Lincoln Park Coast Cultural District (LPCCD) donated the land for this urban farm. LPCCD is also building eco-friendly housing in the area. Brick City started with $20,000 in seed capital, with Gibbons serving as the lead investor. Since the land wasn't clean enough to host edible vegetation, about half of that initial investment went towards soil and EarthBoxes. These containers circumvent the problem of soil contamination in urban areas, and can produce double yields, despite using less water and fertilizer than conventional gardening. Brick City purchased 500

91

containers at a wholesale cost of $13 each. EarthBox donated another 500. Roughly $3,500 went to purchase soil. The remainder of the startup costs went toward educational resources, tools, seeds and plant materials.

Brick City was certainly fortunate to receive their donations of land and equipment. But it also benefited from a smart business strategy. Brick City's founders approached and won the support of an organization—LPCCD—that is deeply committed to sustainability. They worked hard to mobilize a modest amount of financial and human capital to bring their vision to fruition. They have already lined up a second farm on the rooftop of a neighboring office building, and they are working with the LPCCD to find more land.

Brick City already counts several restaurants as clients, and has sold its crops to residents at $5 a bag. The farm has also donated some of its produce to local pantries and organizations that ensure that the produce reaches the city's poor. This year, [2009] Brick City plans to start a buy-in CSA program, and potentially an on-site farm stand. Longer term, Brick City aims to become a profitable operation, with a presence across all of Newark's five wards. Given that organizations such as local food banks and people like Newark Mayor Cory Booker are expressing a strong desire for more of this kind of produce, it seems likely that Brick City will have no shortage of demand.

MyFarm in San Francisco

MyFarm is a for-profit, decentralized urban farm that grows vegetables in backyard gardens throughout San Francisco. The residents whose backyards house the gardens form the core of MyFarm's customer base. Founder Trevor Paque makes this urban farm even greener than most by using bicycles as the main method of transport. MyFarm also helps customers compost their food scraps in their backyards to enrich their farms.

MyFarm is similar to Brick City in that it manages to avoid paying the considerable premi[ums] for land in the region it

The Value of Urban Farms

Does urban farming have to create a profit? Parks don't turn a profit but they provide valuable environmental services. Urban agriculture has a public health value, can provide a carbon sink, [and] store waste water. These farming spaces can provide a range of hard-to-quantify services.

Josh Viertel, "How to Expand Urban Agriculture," The Dirt, January 28, 2010.

operates [in]. Capital expenditures are also exceptionally low. Gardeners arrive at customers' homes on bikes, with one pulling a trailer full of necessary tools. Sometimes, workers use a truck to deliver a mixture of compost and topsoil. Other than that, the company has a basic website, and engages in a minimal amount of marketing. As a result, the business is essentially a service-based enterprise, and therefore heavily dependent on the cost of labor.

In order to offset those costs, MyFarm charges its customers some hefty premi[ums]: $50 for an initial consultation; $500 to $1,800 for installation; and a $25 weekly maintenance fee. Most customers get a standard 4' × 4' foot raised-bed garden, along with a weekly box of the vegetables harvested from their yard. Customers can also opt for larger gardens in return for a reduction in weekly fees. The extra food allows MyFarm to provide food to other paying customers. MyFarm has been so successful that the company had a waiting list in the hundreds as of October 2008.

City Garden Farms

City Garden Farms is a CSA/cooperative in Portland, Oregon. Dan Bravin and Martin Barrett started City Garden Farms with the goal of growing fresh organic produce without consuming much energy. The business model is similar to MyFarm's, in that both avoid real estate costs by using land owned by others. In City Garden Farms' case, twelve people donate the use of their "unused, underutilized lots, plots, or yards" in exchange for a share of the harvests. (The company's only requirements are that the land be a minimum of 1,000 square feet in size, free from any contamination, and receive eight hours of sunlight a day.) City Garden Farms then sells the remaining produce to nearby consumers through a CSA, as well as at farmers markets.

City Garden shares some similarities with the Brick City model as well. Both employ a farming process called SPIN (small plot intensive), which shuns the traditional, highly mechanized cultivation of rural tracts. City Gardens also started small by focusing on land totaling less than one acre. This allowed City Gardens to keep its startup costs low—probably even lower than Brick City's, since it did not need to purchase the Earth-Boxes and soil.

A Potential for Big Benefits

Urban agriculture can help cities increase food supply, security and quality. With minimal investment, education and training it can also be a non-trivial engine of green-job creation. Entrepreneurs face significant but surmountable obstacles in launching urban farming enterprises. Hundreds of urban farms have sprouted up across the country employing a wide range of business models and practices. A growing number of those designed to be commercially successful are beginning to make a profit—and provide successful models for other entrepreneurs.

With its potential for significant benefits to entrepreneurs, workers and communities, Green For All strongly endorses urban agriculture. We encourage city dwellers with green thumbs and an entrepreneurial spirit to consider it as a profession. Established companies and non-profits have developed techniques, training, and educational programs for the support and benefit of sub-acre farms. Entrepreneurs can use these tools to increase their startups' chances for success.

Bringing urban farming to America's cities is not solely the responsibility of entrepreneurs. Policymakers at the local level must encourage urban farming in the underutilized areas of their cities. They can do this by relaxing any zoning or land-use restrictions that might impede urban agriculture. Perhaps more importantly, cities owning blighted land can lease it long-term to urban farmers. Given the civic benefits of urban agriculture, these leases should ideally be for next to nothing. Local banks and other financial intermediaries have a part to play, as well. They can support urban agriculture by loosening their purse strings and providing low-cost loans to urban farms that convincingly demonstrate the viability of their business models.

With entrepreneurs, policymakers and financial institutions working together, we can expand urban agriculture in America, increasing food safety, security and quality while creating new jobs and wealth in struggling communities.

"*Farming is generally a business . . . and when you don't treat it as a business, it fails.*"

Urban Agriculture Is Sustainable If Treated as a Legitimate Business

Isaiah Thompson

Isaiah Thompson is news editor at the Philadelphia City Paper. *In the following viewpoint, Thompson explores Philadelphia's roots in urban farming in the 1970s, questions the causes of the movement's decline, and contends that, with the help and encouragement of the city's Redevelopment Authority, there is no reason for urban agriculture not to thrive as a legitimate business venture, even in the "half-blighted, post-industrial" areas of the city. Additionally, says Thompson, Philadelphia's Department of Parks and Recreation must agree to lease out park land for agriculture, which, Thompson adds, would be far more amenable to farming than vacant lots and brownfield sites that are heavily polluted and require more serious cleanup and soil improvement. Ultimately, Thompson maintains, urban farming must prove itself profitable to be accepted and encouraged by local urban government and policy makers.*

As you read, consider the following questions:

1. According to Thompson, what is the main problem facing urban agriculture in Philadelphia?
2. Which US government agency funded an early example of urban farming in Philadelphia, according to the author?
3. Which population does Thompson indicate has been best served by Philadelphia's urban farms?

A few weeks ago, at a community meeting in North Philadelphia, I witnessed a scene that seemed somehow symbolic, prophetic, even. The meeting—an energized rally by the Eastern North Philadelphia Coalition, a group trying to acquire vacant land for a neighborhood-managed land trust—had just ended, and community members were filing out.

At the door was a young, bearded white guy, passing out seeds.

"Free seeds!" he shouted jubilantly. "Take them home, plant them, have better food, save money!"

It seemed to embody in a single moment all the hope, passion—and, frankly, dubiousness—of the urban agriculture movement that is sweeping Philadelphia.

There's nothing radical about the idea of raising edible crops in the city: It's been done for ages. And Philadelphia, it cannot be denied, has plenty of land—including thousands of vacant lots.

What is a little more dubious is the sheer distance between what urban agriculture's most idealistic proponents want it to mean to Philadelphia—a self-sufficient means of food production for the poor, a source of jobs, a cure for the ills of urban obesity and malnutrition—and its reality on the ground so far.

Whether that distance can be breached may be put to the test soon. In recent years, urban agriculture has had the luxury of defining itself in opposition: to a culture of cheap, pesticide-dependent produce; to a society increasingly isolated from and ignorant of the origin of its food; and to a city which has sometimes seen vegetable gardens on vacant lots as impeding development—rather than vice versa.

But about a year ago [in 2009], something surprising happened: The city itself began to get all . . . *urban aggy*, with various city agencies coming up with proposals to sponsor new inner-city farms. Urban agriculture, all of a sudden, is in. The problem, quickly becoming apparent, is that no one quite agrees on what, exactly, it's supposed to be.

Urban Farming in the 1970s

If the idea of Philadelphia—half-blighted, post-industrial, faded-glory Philly—as an urban gardening mecca seems wildly optimistic, it's worth noting that, not long ago, it was already well on its way. The 1970s marked a heyday of Philadelphia urban farming. As industrial jobs left and vacant lots sprang up around the city, urban gardens took off—tilled largely by Southern-born black and immigrant communities, many of whom had grown up raising vegetables. They had support, too. The Philadelphia Horticultural Society's "Philadelphia Green" program helped prospective farmers get access to land. Penn State's newly formed Urban Gardening program made Philadelphia a centerpiece of a six-city pilot program later adopted and funded by the USDA [United States Department of Agriculture].

These gardens, according to research by University of Pennsylvania planning professor Domenic Vitiello, thrived into the 1990s. In 1994, he notes in a 2008 report, Penn State's program knew of 501 area gardens maintained by an estimated 2,800 families that produced nearly $2 million worth of fruits and vegetables.

But within the span of 10 years, many vanished. In 1996, the USDA cut funding for urban gardening. Penn State and the Horticultural Society began to redirect their efforts away from urban agriculture. Gardeners themselves got older or passed away. And—good news to many—property values began to rise. Some gardens were replaced with development; others, according to Vitiello's research team, were quietly shut down by city officials.

Many are still alive and kicking—and the nonprofit Neighborhood Gardens Association has made its mission the preservation of these places by placing them in its land trust.

. "At this point we have 30 gardens," says executive director Terry Mushovic, "and about 96 percent of that is food production."

Some of the biggest and most active gardens, she says, are powered by immigrants from Southeast Asia and Latin America: "They are growing massively," she says. "It's no hobby."

But there's no question such gardens have declined overall. Of the 600-odd former program-supported garden sites surveyed by Vitiello's team, 255 were inactive, and more than half of those are now vacant lots.

To Vitiello and many others, the story's moral is clear: With support from Philadelphia institutions, and from the city itself, urban agriculture in Philadelphia can thrive again—it just needs a hand up, and maybe a handout, too.

Encountering Bureaucracy

And if Vitiello has become the academic voice of that argument in Philadelphia, a new wave of urban ag enthusiasts—mostly young, white and educated—have become its arms and legs, lobbying the city to hand over what they see as the missing piece of the puzzle: "The biggest road block people like us have is access to land," says Matt McFarland, who owns a burgeoning half-acre urban farm with his wife, Amanda, in Germantown. "It's not really viable for us to be buying land in competition with regular development."

Until recently, the city hadn't shown much interest in handing over land for gardening. But the aggies are dangling a new carrot before the city. They want to make urban agriculture a business; they want to make money doing this.

Multifunctional Farms

Farms produce more than food for consumers and money for farmers. To employ a phrase from economics, they are multifunctional: they produce food, yes, but also environmental goods like healthy soil (or damages like depleted soil and polluted waterways); open, pretty spaces for the public (or public nuisances, as in the case of factory-scale animal farms). The problem is that they only get paid for the food—and not nearly enough, many people now agree.

Tom Philpott, "Urban Farms Don't Make Money—So What?," Grist, June 3, 2010.

It seems to be this new orientation that finally caught the city's interest. Giving away developable land for private gardening is one thing,but supporting "green business," maybe even creating "green jobs"? Hello, Zeitgeist!

The city Redevelopment Authority (RDA) was the first agency to reach for the torch, announcing last year it would be issuing a Request for Proposal to do commercial greenhouse gardening on a long-vacant parcel it held. A few months later, Mayor Michael Nutter announced his ambitious Greenworks Philadelphia plan that was supposed to make Philadelphia "the greenest city in America." Among its many goals: establishing 12 new urban farms and 15 new farmers markets by 2015.

But not long after the RDA's request for proposals was issued, it was withdrawn, and the RDA backed off abruptly.

Terry Gillen, RDA's executive director, characterizes the misstep as a simple need for more time, more planning, more research: "What we found is it was way more complicated than we thought," says Gillen. "We realized there was a lot we didn't know, and we wanted to go back to the drawing board."

But urban aggers counter that the RDA was dipping its toes where it feared to swim, blaming an institutional nervousness when it comes to giving up control of any land.

"[Gillen] really wanted to develop an interim land-usage program—and it's an open debate as to whether you can build something and operate something in the three- to five-year period the RDA wanted to lease the land for," points out Mary Seton Corboy, co-founder of Greensgrow Farm, which was itself built 13 years ago on RDA-leased land, and represents one of the only economically successful urban "farms" in the city.

"Gillen saw it as a way the RDA could get land off its hands but still manage long-term control over it," Corboy explains. "Other people said, that's ridiculous, you need to give someone a minimum of 10 years."

Farming As a Business

The next city agency to give urban agriculture a shot is the Department of Parks and Recreation, which has unveiled a plan to lease out park land in the Manatawna Farms area—much easier to farm than vacant lots and brownfields—for for-profit commercial farming. The department has issued a Request for Information, to be followed by a Request for Proposal, to lease out 10 half-acre plots to willing farmers at a nominal price.

"What we're hoping to demonstrate is you don't need large parcels of land, that this is a viable economic process," says Environment, Stewardship and Education director Joan Blaustein. This idea has met with a warmer reception from urban ag gurus.

"Farming is generally a business and it has to be treated like a business," says Greensgrow's Corboy, "and when you don't treat it as a business, it fails."

Roxanne Christensen, co-founder of Somerton Tanks Farm, a now-finished demonstration project which also used public land to create a for-profit urban farm, agrees. She says the distinction between profitable and nonprofit farming is everything:

"It's a distinction I harp on, and that I think is important," says Christensen. "It's the only way urban agriculture is going to be established on any scale."

Reconciling Business and Community Needs

But the profitable end of urban gardening has so far catered largely to the recent, and decidedly upper-end, market for higher-priced local food—which puts a few holes in the sails of those who tout it as a solution to the needs of poor city residents.

The nonprofit Mill Creek Farm, for example, serves a largely educational function for low-income neighbors, according to co-director Jade Walker (although they do donate to the local food bank). She sees the city's best role as preserving existing community farms, rather than actively pursuing new ones.

"I'd like to say it's not a separate issue," admits Christensen, referring to the lofty goals of inner-city low-income food access and nutrition, "but how urban agriculture can address that, when farmers have to make a living, I don't know. I think we'll see how—maybe that sounds like a cop-out, but I really think so.

"See if there's any interest in people becoming farmers in those [low-income] areas," she adds. "They'll figure out how to serve their markets."

"In a city where the swaths of abandonment seem to grow by the day, entrepreneurs and public officials are seeing a chance to capitalize on blight by turning wasteland into farmland."

Cleveland's For-Profit Urban Gardens Are Growing

Marty Sterpka

Marty Sterpka is a news editor at the Cleveland Plain Dealer, *an Ohio daily newspaper. In the following viewpoint, Sterpka examines the proliferation of urban gardens in Cleveland, one of the most economically depressed big cities in the United States. With an unofficial count of more than two hundred community gardens growing on the city's numerous empty lots, Sterpka explains, many of those farmers have been able to turn a profit on their enterprises, which were initially intended to help beautify a blighted landscape and bring much-needed nutritional value to the food-insecure. According to Sterpka, urban farming specialists agree that, with the right crops and growing procedures, even farmers of half-acre plots are capable of earning a relatively large return on their investments, and the possibility is ripe for urban farming to shoot to the top of Cleveland's industrial base. One major challenge to turning small farms into large-scale business success, says Sterpka, lies in* marketing. *Without the commitment of city institutions such as hospitals, schools, supermarkets, and others to buy locally grown produce on a greater scale, Sterpka asserts, Cleveland's urban farmers will continue to find themselves in a small market where production outpaces demand.*

As you read, consider the following questions:
1. According to the author, what are the potential economic advantages of urban agriculture for a city like Cleveland?
2. What does Sterpka say is the average distance food travels from "farm to plate"?
3. About how many vacant acres are in Cleveland, according to the author?

Cleveland, Ohio—Money doesn't grow on trees, we've been told our whole lives.

But it might grow on vacant lots all over Cleveland.

More on Urban Gardens

It could grow in row upon row of beans, tomatoes, herbs and strawberries planted on deserted land and between deserted buildings—and in fact it already is. Gardeners who have cultivated food on derelict land for themselves and their friends are now growing food to sell for profit.

In a city where the swaths of abandonment seem to grow by the day, entrepreneurs and public officials are seeing a chance to capitalize on blight by turning wasteland into farmland.

No single entity keeps comprehensive tabs on the scale and scope. Yet, leaders of various gardening programs say the city is seeing what they believe is its biggest proliferation of big-lot gardens since the Victory Garden days of World War II.

By various counts, more than 200 community gardens—neighborhood grow-your-own collaborations—have sprung up on empty lots. Scores of community-gardening enthusiasts are graduating to tending "market gardens"—for-profit enterprises trying to make a go of it as side businesses. About a dozen entrepreneurs have made it a full-time job—a career.

Wind and solar energy and biotech frontiers grab headlines and venture capital as "green jobs" generators. But a loose coalition of enthusiasts ranging from dirt farmers to top elected officials and civic leaders see raising and marketing of fresh, local produce on idle lots as a realistic vehicle for green job creation, entrepreneurship and revitalization.

"What's going on is agriculture—but it's really economic development," said Natalie Ronayne, executive director of the Cleveland Botanical Garden.

City Ready for Economic Growth

Someday, and maybe soon, those opportunities could create hundreds of small farms—each a small business providing a livelihood for one or more people—within city limits.

It's enticing on a micro level, says Morgan Taggart, an urban-farming specialist at Ohio State University's Cuyahoga County extension service.

"There definitely can be a good return on investment," she said.

How good? Researchers at OSU's Ohio Agricultural Research and Development Center estimate that urban farmers could gross up to $90,000 per acre by selecting the right crops and growing techniques, Taggart said. At experimental plots in Philadelphia, urban-market gardeners pulled in up to $68,000 in revenue per half-acre.

Then there's the big-picture, macroeconomic appeal: The effort could mean hundreds of millions of dollars to Cleveland's economy each year, enough to land farming among the city's biggest industries.

By one estimate, Northeast Ohioans annually spend $7 billion on food—Clevelanders accounting for about $1 billion of that—and less than 5 percent is produced locally. Most is shipped here from far away—an average trip of 1,300 miles from farm to plate. Consequently, billions of dollars flow out of our local economy and into the pockets of farmers and industrial conglomerates far, far away.

If Northeast Ohio could grow its local food-production industry enough to recapture just a few percent more of that, "that's hundreds of millions of dollars that can be captured here," said Bradley Whitehead, who heads the Fund for Our Economic Future.

Whitehead's economic-development organization is intertwined with the region's major chambers of commerce and is funded by mainstream business and philanthropic interests here.

Some people point to the fund's fascination, and its willingness to invest $200,000 or more into studying ways to better market locally grown food, as a sign that local urban agriculture's shoots have reached the establishment.

"Ten years ago, there were only a handful of people doing this," observed Brad Masi, a local-foods activist, farmer and teacher at Oberlin College's New Agrarian Center. "In the last two years, we've seen just an explosion.

"What's driving the whole thing," Masi added, "is that entrepreneurial people are creating their own opportunities."

And there is a lot of help.

Ronayne's University Circle nonprofit has been teaching gardeners for 70 years. Its fast-growing Green Corps Urban Youth Program employs about 80 people, mostly teenagers, to run a half-dozen inner-city farms of an acre or less each.

Some of its former garden managers have created careers as the Johnny Appleseeds of for-profit urban farming, teaching others to scratch out a living—or at least a side income—from the urban soil.

Joining them are denim-overalls agriculture experts from OSU, Case Western Reserve University and Oberlin and, in a recent twist, Whitehead and other backers from the suit-and-tie world of Greater Cleveland's economic-development establishment. A business-leadership coalition called Entrepreneurs for Sustainability has added to the momentum.

Urban Farmers Face Opportunities and Obstacles

Opportunities already abound, says OSU's Taggart.

"You don't need a ton of infrastructure to produce food," she said. "You need access to land, water, sun and know-how. That's not a lot of barriers to entry compared to other start-ups."

Certainly, access to open land gives Cleveland a leg up— albeit perversely: Decades of population drain, industrial death and, most recently, the foreclosure crisis have left about 3,300 vacant acres in the city, and at least 15,000 vacant buildings.

A report last fall for the nonprofit Neighborhood Progress Inc. and the Cleveland Planning Commission cast those sobering figures in a most optimistic light, particularly for city farming.

"After demolition," the report heralded, "surplus land becomes a raw asset for the city—a resource for future development as the city's population stabilizes and progress is made toward recovery."

Cuyahoga County Treasurer Jim Rokakis recently led the creation of a quasi-government land-bank agency to recycle that land and now is trying to issue bonds for redevelopment—a vision that includes small-business financing for urban farmers.

"We can take these problem properties and turn them into opportunities," he said. "I really believe that."

But there are many hurdles to overcome, Rokakis and Taggart agree. A big challenge: finding ways to sell a lot more locally grown food.

The markets are good now—growing demand and limited competition on the supply side, many growers say.

Customers at the ever-expanding number of local farmers markets are snapping up so much of what grows in the city that the gourmet chefs who also demand local produce can scarcely get enough.

City farmers are also selling through "community-supported agriculture" arrangements, under which fresh-food fans pre-pay in the winter for weekly deliveries of whatever fresh crops are in season during the spring, summer and fall.

But those mechanisms would support only some small percentage of growth in supply. For urban gardeners to green up hundreds more acres of the city's blighted core and really boost the local economy, their market needs to grow.

That kind of market development is Peter McDermott's job working for the Entrepreneurs for Sustainability business group, and he says it's not an easy task.

"It's a chicken-and-egg question," McDermott said.

Success, McDermott explained, would mean getting major institutions—hospitals, schools, supermarkets and more—to commit at a far greater scale to buying local produce. That can be a difficult proposition to sell, given that local food fetches high prices now, while demand outstrips supply.

Without a bigger, established market, it could be difficult to recruit banks to invest in start-up loans or other capital needs, added Rokakis. He has a list of more than 700 vacant properties of a quarter-acre or more, and scores of them would be ideal for high-intensity farms.

"It's doable, but it's not going to be easy," Rokakis said. "We need to create a market for local products here. I don't think it's going to happen overnight.

"I think there is a model out there," he added. "We just have to find it."

> "Although popularity and trendiness can be big boons to business, urban farms haven't yet found a way to thrive in the market economy."

Urban Agriculture Accounts for a Small but Important Segment of the Sustainable Food Market

Sena Christian

Sena Christian is a journalist based in Sacramento, California, who specializes in environmental and social justice issues. In the following viewpoint, Christian addresses the question of the ability of urban farms in American cities to grow and market food on a scale broad enough to make a difference in a city's or region's larger economy. The problem, Christian says, is that too many urban farms are unable to achieve financial self-sufficiency and instead have to rely on funds from foundations and grants. Another problem Christian points to is access to land. Vacant and abandoned properties typically are city-owned, she explains, and city governments usually prefer to hold on to such properties for development opportunities rather than lend or sell them for the purpose of farming. Yet Christian notes that even impoverished cities maintain large food economies, simply because residents have to eat, one way or another. Citing a 2008 study, Christian writes that when large proportions of food spending are spent on nonlocally produced food, tens of millions of dollars in potential revenue are lost from the local economy.

As you read, consider the following questions:

1. How does the author indicate that City Slicker Farms addresses its customers' varying abilities to pay?
2. What is a major obstacle to urban farming success, according to Christian?
3. What does Christian maintain that urban farms must do to meet demand and compete in the marketplace?

Although part of the broader sustainable food phenomenon, many of the country's urban farms seek to tackle issues that Whole Foods, with its relatively high prices and affluent customers, is not addressing. The urban farm movement aims to take control of food production away from large-scale industrial agriculture and root it within local food systems that attempt to ensure food access for the urban poor. Often located in low-income neighborhoods, many city farms operate off the basic premise that healthy, affordable food is a basic human right. "Food justice" is the mantra of most, if not all, of the organizations in the urban farming movement. That means serving the estimated 14 percent of Americans who experience food insecurity—49 million people who are unsure where they'll find their next meal.

Yet urban farming's potential to address the challenges of our food system remains unclear. Although popularity and trendiness can be big boons to business, these urban farms haven't yet found a way to thrive in the market economy. Most rely heavily on volunteer labor and grant funding. They may be at the forefront of ecological sustainability, but economic sustainability eludes them. And that's a problem because they are unlikely to fulfill their aspirations and make a meaningful dent in the problem of food insecurity if they are forever running on the treadmill of foundation funding.

"The most fundamental question is about scale," says Brahm Ahmadi, co-founder of People's Grocery in Oakland [California].

By "scale" Ahmadi means the ability of urban farming projects to satisfy the demand for sustainable food that exists in a given community. According to Ahmadi, in many food-insecure neighborhoods 60 to 70 percent of food dollars are spent outside the community. Most urban farms are able to close only a fraction of that gap, about 10 percent.

"If we're going to address food justice to make any significant effect on this massive issue, we're going to have to scale different," Ahmadi says.

Let Them Eat Kale

On this Friday morning, the workers at Soil Born Farms gather arugula—an item planted at the request of a local chef at a fancy restaurant. Arugula will also be added to the farm's community-supported agriculture (CSA) boxes, along with collards, chard, beets, carrots, mustard greens, and broccoli. A couple of teenagers help harvest vegetables. They earn $8 an hour to work about 20 hours a week as part of the organization's Green Corps program to provide job training to local youth.

After harvesting, the group lines up boxes on a long table and unloads crates of produce. A cow moos. Soil Born Farms has seven sheep, 11 lambs, 80 chickens (that lay eggs to sell at the farm stand), four cows, and one pig that roams around aimlessly. A few yards away, Porter the dog runs through the fields. He keeps coyotes at bay. While the farm is adjacent to commercial and residential buildings on one side, the American River flows down the other side of the farm, offering a touch of wildness.

During winter, Soil Born harvests two days a week to fill 60 CSA boxes—80 boxes in the summer. In a CSA, consumers pay for their weekly produce boxes in advance of the growing season, which gives farms a cushion from market forces and unpredictable weather, and provides consumers with food from a source they can trust.

This is Soil Born's first attempt at a winter CSA program. The expansion is intended to raise funds and please customers who want local produce year-round. "We'll make it," Hagan says of the experiment. "But it's going to be close."

Soil Born Farms began as a small for-profit farm in 2000. In 2004, it transitioned into a nonprofit organization. "The plan was always to morph into an urban farm and education center that best addressed the diverse issues: food education, production, and improved access to healthy foods," says Soil Born Farms co-founder Shawn Harrison. "Once we determined that we had the capacity and ability to grow food and be good farmers—[co-founder] Marco Franciosa and I did not grow up in farming—becoming a nonprofit was the natural choice."

Harrison and Franciosa determined that in order to tap into community and foundation financial support, and more easily access public-land resources, becoming a nonprofit organization made the most sense.

In addition to the CSA, Soil Born runs a farm stand and sells food to restaurants. The farm also has an explicit social mission. It organizes a volunteer fruit-gleaning group, which donated nearly 20,000 pounds of produce to local food banks in 2009, and serves 1,500 children a year through its educational programs. Staff members also work closely with the city's large Hmong community to increase market opportunities for Southeast Asian growers. Balancing farming responsibilities with time-consuming educational programs can be challenging. . . .

The organization is doing its best to sustain itself through sales, which isn't easy. In 2009, the organization's budget was $780,000; the 2010 budget is about $1 million. Nearly 60 percent of the organization's revenue comes from private foundations and government grants. What Soil Born Farms could use, the managers acknowledge, is a big revenue-generating idea.

"We've yet to make the farm self-sufficient," Hagan says. "I think we're close." . . .

Gardening as Self-Sufficiency

On a Saturday morning in March, neighbors congregate for a weekly farm stand in front of one of City Slicker Farms' seven garden sites. Customers try samples from a plate of honey while bagging up carrots and bok choy, self-determining what price they can afford. The organization uses sliding scale pricing so no one is turned away for lack of funds. The first level is for those out of work whose unemployment check maybe hasn't yet arrived—City Slicker Farms asks for no explanation—and these people get carrots, lemons, collards, celery, and other items for free. The second level is intended for people living paycheck-to-paycheck who would otherwise search for deals at Safeway [a western United States grocery chain]; they pay between 50 cents and $1.25 for a bunch of greens or a bag of carrots. The third level is for people who can afford to shop at Whole Foods but would rather support the farm stand and can afford to pay a little more. They pay between around $2 for a bag or bunch. . . .

City Slicker Farms hosts a backyard garden build every Saturday for low-income residents. It's like a traditional barn-raising, with everyone and anyone in the neighborhood invited to chip in. Participants in the program help build their garden beds, with soil, plants, seeds, and a fruit tree donated by the organization. For two years, a garden mentor provides horticulture advice to participants. Since the program started in 2005, the organization has built 112 gardens; 99 of those families remain involved.

As morning turns into afternoon, Abeni Ramsey, the group's market coordinator, walks through the garden behind the farm stand, the place where it all started in 2001. Now the site acts more as a demonstration garden, with a worm bin, an outdoor classroom, and growing tubes that sprout parsley, green onions, and celery. Every summer growing up, Ramsey traveled from

Berkeley to Queens, New York, to help her grandfather prune tomatoes and harvest corn at his urban farm. About a decade ago, Ramsey recalls, the only grocery store in West Oakland closed down.

"I had a hard time getting access to healthy fruits and veggies," Ramsey says. One day, she biked through the neighborhood and saw signs for City Slicker Farms. "I couldn't believe someone was advertising fresh produce in West Oakland."

Before long, the organization [had] built two garden boxes in the shambles of a backyard behind her old Victorian house. Later, she acquired chickens and goats, recognizing that the once-empty space could provide food for her whole family.

"Just because [West Oakland] looks like a barren wasteland, it doesn't have to be like that," says Ramsey, who serves as one of City Slicker Farms' eight staff members.

Investigating Land Ownership

As Ramsey and [City Slicker Farms executive director Barbara] Finnin visit with neighbors, two young men venture up to the farm stand, one holding a video camera and the other air-monitoring equipment. They're part of a youth media group investigating the Bay Area's "Toxic Triangle": San Francisco's naval shipyard, Richmond's Chevron refinery, and the Port of Oakland.

The air pollution and lead in the soil in parts of many US cities compound another critical roadblock for food-access folks: the lack of land available for urban farming. City Slicker Farms doesn't own any of the land upon which it grows. Neither does Soil Born Farms. Finnin wants the city of Oakland to allocate land specifically for agricultural use. She wants the city to repurpose parks and turn them into edible gardens.

The group's long-term vision involves West Oakland growing 40 percent of its own fruits and vegetables. City Slicker staff estimate that meeting that goal would require 77 acres of land, or 3 percent of the community's total area.

Old Movement, New Technology

While . . . innovations [in urban agriculture] are based on historical precedents, from the radical Diggers movement of 17th century Britain, to sharecropping arrangements, the victory garden movements during the World Wars, and recent community supported agriculture systems, they are unique in that they apply social networking tools, mapping technologies, unusual land tenure arrangements, or novel business models to forage and farm cities and suburbs.

Nevin Cohen, "Models of Distributed Urban Agriculture," Civil Eats, July 9, 2009. www.civileats.com.

"We're trying to build capacity for self-sufficiency," Finnin says. "We want this to scale."

City Slicker Farms' food-justice mission is driven by the ideal of neighborhood empowerment: Teaching local residents how to garden and feed themselves.

But City Slicker Farms, like Soil Born, faces the classic challenge of nonprofit organizations—a dependence on grants. The question remains: How can City Slicker Farms get bigger? It's the same problem faced by most urban farms and food-access organizations.

Take, for example, Milwaukee's Growing Power, widely recognized as one of the most impressive urban farms in the country. Growing Power operates 14 greenhouses situated on two acres in a working-class neighborhood, near the city's largest public-housing project. The farm produces a quarter of a million dollars' worth of food a year, which feeds 10,000 residents through an on-farm retail store, restaurants, schools, farmers' markets, and low-cost CSA shares. Founder Will Allen, whose father was a sharecropper in South Carolina, started the organization in 1993.

In 2009, he was honored with a MacArthur "genius" award. Allen uses millions of pounds of food waste as compost—some of which is sold—and plants seeds at quadruple density to maximize space. From a sustainable-agriculture standpoint, Growing Power is a success. But it's not financially self-sufficient. In the past five years, Allen has received at least $1 million in grants.

Produce to the People

People's Grocery, another food justice organization based in West Oakland, believes it has a plan to be both economically self-sufficient and meet its core goal of increasing food access for low-income households: opening up its own neighborhood grocery store.

In 2003, the organization started distributing organic food in the area with its "mobile market"—a mediagenic biodiesel-powered, brightly painted converted postal van that cruised the neighborhood, stopping on corners to sell all the offerings one could find in a typical health food store. While the effort was a huge success in terms of public education, it was a financial drain. Sixty percent of the market's revenue came from philanthropies, and the organization shuttered the van in 2006.

Since then, People's Grocery has pivoted its focus to food production. The organization has two garden sites in Oakland and a 3.5-acre farm 35 miles away. Its CSA program—called GRUB—serves roughly 300 customers. Like City Slicker Farms, People's Grocery has a graduated pricing system. People on food stamps, or those suffering from chronic disease, pay a discounted rate, while more affluent customers can purchase a "sponsorship box" at a premium rate to subsidize the program's costs. The GRUB boxes generate close to $50,000 a year in revenue, but People's Grocery remains reliant on donations and grants. . . .

A Huge Food Economy

Not a single large grocery store exists in West Oakland, a neighborhood of about 24,000 people covering five square miles. But some 50 corner stores operate there, which equates to about one store for every 500 residents, as opposed to the middle-class neighborhoods of Oakland where one corner store exists for every 7,000 people, according to Ahmadi. Additionally, he says, corner stores charge 30 to 100 percent more for the same items sold in grocery stores.

A 2008 study found that West Oakland residents spend about $54 million annually for food for at-home consumption. Sixty-eight percent of this annual expenditure is not met locally, which equates to almost $37 million lost from the local economy. Or, put another way, even in this relatively poor neighborhood there's a $50 million food economy, which means there should be some way for the economics to pencil out for a sustainable food operation.

After that study came out, Ahmadi totaled the revenues and weight of food distributed by five West Oakland food-access organizations—including People's Grocery and City Slicker Farms—and compared those to the identified food-spending power. Together, the organizations' total activities met about 1 percent of the community's demand.

"That was a very humbling experience, and a very important moment for me to realize how far we have to go," Ahmadi says. "We have to scale, that's the bottom line."

The Logistics of Local Food

To reach a scale that can meet demand, food access organizations have to offer a broad selection of products, large quantities of those products, accessible locations, and convenient operating hours—the same basics that customers at Whole Foods in the more upscale city of Berkeley expect—with the added bonus of affordable prices.

"Low-income residents want full selection across a broad array of categories, which is why they spend a lot of time, money, and effort traveling to outlying grocery stores that are large enough to offer a suitable selection," Ahmadi says.

The group is about to start lease negotiations on a site that was once a popular shopping center. And Ahmadi believes he can leverage the nonprofit's history of success to attract investors. The store, to be called People's Community Market, is set to launch in early 2011. [It was still not yet open in September 2011.]

Growing Profits

As even its ardent protagonists acknowledge, city farming's potential is limited. The United States' small-scale city farm projects are micro-enterprises with modest revenue and distribution. They provide an important entry point for city dwellers to learn about the need for sustainable food systems, but they will never feed the country. . . .

The best strategy for urban farm organizations might be to simply let the fruits and vegetables speak for themselves. At least, that's the approach taken by Greensgrow, an urban farm started in 1998 in a low-income neighborhood of north Philadelphia, that has figured out how to both turn a profit and make local organic produce available to nearby residents. The organization has a one-acre plot of raised beds and greenhouses on the site of a former steel-galvanizing factory. It sells vegetables, herbs, honey, and seedlings produced on-site, along with produce, breads, meats, and cheeses from local producers. Greensgrow also makes biodiesel from waste oil produced by the restaurants that buy its vegetables.

"We are extremely diversified," says co-founder Mary Seton Corboy. She says this diversification partly explains why her organization is financially self-sufficient, while many other urban farms are not. In 2009, Greensgrow had an income of $825,000. That's earned income from CSAs, farm stand sales, restaurant sales, and nursery sales. Their profit of $85,000 was then invested in community programs, including workshops, tour visits, and plant giveaways. . . .

Greensgrow is, technically, a nonprofit. The group recently started a community kitchen and received $20,000 in grants to cover initial costs. The farm is starting a low-income CSA later this year [2010], and because there's an educational component to the program, the organization is looking for outside funding. But with a social mission focused on incubating ecological entrepreneurship, Greensgrow has always operated as if it were a for-profit company. . . .

| "City of Detroit officials are struggling to understand the implications of urban agriculture within city limits."

Commercial Urban Agriculture Faces Political Barriers

John Gallagher

John Gallagher is a business writer for the Detroit Free Press. In the following viewpoint, Gallagher assesses the state of large-scale commercial farming proposals in the city of Detroit, concluding that the slow decision making of city politicians is resulting in frustration and anger among entrepreneurs whose projects have been stymied. According to Gallagher, the administration of Mayor Dave Bing is overly cautious about investing heavily in urban agriculture partly because of unclear zoning restrictions that may or may not restrict the growing of food within city limits. But beyond that, says Gallagher, Michigan's Right to Farm law may contain language that inadvertently allows large corporations to avoid city regulations after approval. Additionally, Gallagher declares, many Detroit residents and owners of already existing nonprofit farms in the city view one such corporation with suspicion, considering it more interested in buying up as much city land as possible at the *lowest prices possible with little or no intention of spreading the economic benefits to city residents once its planned farm becomes profitable.*

As you read, consider the following questions:

1. What does Gary Wozniak, as cited by Gallagher, see as the city's main problem with approving agricultural plans?
2. How many acres does John Hantz hope to farm in Detroit, according to the author?
3. How many square miles of vacant land does Gallagher say are currently in the city of Detroit?

To farm or not farm? That's Detroit's question.

A city already filled with tiny community gardens so far has balked at allowing larger-scale commercial farming inside the city. Several such farm projects have been proposed for more than a year, but as 2010 winds down, they still await city approval.

Some of the would-be urban growers are letting their frustration show.

"There's always another layer of the onion we have to peel, and quite honestly I don't understand it," said Gary Wozniak, director of the proposed RecoveryPark project, which would initially farm about 20 acres on Detroit's east side. "Every time they overcome another hurdle, there's another hurdle."

Dan Lijana, a spokesman for Mayor Dave Bing, said urban agriculture is just one of many ideas the city is weighing as part of Bing's Detroit Works plan to reinvent the city.

"Mayor Bing continues to be receptive to all ideas for economic development, including commercial urban farming," Lijana said. "While no announcement is imminent, conversations and progress continue."

Corporate vs. Grassroots Farming

[Corporation owner John Hantz] doesn't have many fans among the community gardeners [in Detroit], who feel that Hantz is using his money and connections to capitalize on their pioneering work. "I'm concerned about the corporate takeover of the urban agriculture movement in Detroit," says Malik Yakini, a charter school principal and founder of the Detroit Black Community Food Security Network, which operates D-Town Farm on Detroit's west side. "At this point the key players with him seem to be all white men in a city that's at least 82% black."

David Whitford, "Can Farming
Save Detroit?," Fortune Magazine,
December 29, 2009.

Commercial Urban Farms Delayed

As last spring's growing season began, 2010 looked like the year when Detroiters would undertake bold experiments in large-scale commercial urban agriculture in the city.

But as 2010's growing season ends, not one of four such projects on the table last spring has broken ground yet.

Some of the projects now hope to get in the ground next spring, but even that is uncertain. City of Detroit officials are struggling to understand the implications of urban agriculture within city limits. Among the concerns holding up approval are worries about noise and pollution, a lack of zoning for growing food in the city, and questions over who benefits from any economic gain.

Gary Wozniak, project director of RecoveryPark, a nonprofit venture that hopes to begin large-scale farming on Detroit's east side soon, is frustrated by the delays in winning approval for his project.

"I think the problem is the city doesn't want to make a decision, quite honestly," Wozniak said. "Every time we think we've reached a certain plateau, we get another excuse. . . . We should be taking risks. We should be looking at this as opportunities."

Dan Lijana, a spokesman for Mayor Dave Bing, said the city will not be rushed as it considers projects like RecoveryPark.

RecoveryPark would initially farm about 20 acres near Warren and Chene on the east side, on vacant land owned by Detroit Public Schools. But the project still needs approval from the city, and city approval is not yet forthcoming.

Other Projects Await Approval

Meanwhile, Detroit businessman John Hantz had proposed his Hantz Farms project in early 2009, hoping to farm some 2,000 acres of vacant city-owned land. As of this fall [2010], he was reportedly going to get about 100 acres of city-owned vacant land on the east side near the Indian Village district to begin commercial farming.

But with Bing's ambitious Detroit Works project to rethink the city still in its early stages, no decision is expected now on Hantz's proposal until next spring [2011] at the earliest. A spokeswoman for Hantz declined to comment.

In another project, New York City activist Majora Carter had sought a Kresge Foundation grant to establish a farmers cooperative in Detroit that would produce jobs and revenue for the city. But Kresge turned down her application pending some decision from the Bing administration on commercial farming.

In a fourth project, the nonprofit Greening of Detroit has purchased 2.5 acres near Eastern Market to operate a farm and training facility to teach community gardeners how to turn their small, local farms into revenue generators. But bureaucratic delays at various levels have delayed groundbreaking from this year to next.

An Untested Industry

Dan Carmody, president of the nonprofit Eastern Market Corp., supports a more localized food system, but he said some delays are understandable, given the complexities of the issues.

"It's a new kind of industry, and there are some growing pains associated with it," Carmody said.

Wozniak is project director for a drug rehabilitation agency called SHAR that is undertaking RecoveryPark. The project would put recovering addicts and other distressed individuals to work growing crops and processing food.

In a city with an estimated 40 square miles of vacant land, Wozniak said, the city ought to be willing to experiment with a relatively small project like RecoveryPark.

"Everybody's doing all these projects in other cities," Wozniak said. "They're all looking at Detroit. They're all looking for us for the ideas we're going to create, and we're not creating any."

Small-scale, volunteer community gardens already exist all over Detroit. But city officials cite various issues that need to be overcome before they can approve larger-scale commercial farming in the city.

Unclear Laws and Growing Frustration

For one thing, there still is no zoning classification for growing food inside the city. Officials also are worried that Michigan's Right to Farm law, which protects rural farmers against the encroachments of suburban sprawl, might be used by businessmen like Hantz to avoid regulation by the city after initial approval is given.

Then, too, many of Detroit's nonprofit community gardeners are urging the city to reject Hantz's proposal, viewing for-profit farming in the city as exploitation and a land grab. Critics worry that ordinary citizens won't benefit if profits go mainly to wealthy business owners.

Whatever the reasons, the delays are leaving Wozniak and others frustrated.

"We've asked the city for no money, no tax breaks, no resources other than access to land," he said. "And we don't care if we buy it, lease it, if it's deeded to us, if it's in a trust. Let us try something."

| "It is becoming possible to compete with big food, producing organic, transport-free, cross-seasonal produce, within the most urban of places."

Urban Farms Can Compete Economically with Industrial Agriculture

Mike Duff

Mike Duff works at Happold Consulting in the area of urban strategy, planning, and sustainability. He also is a guest lecturer for the Bartlett School of Architecture at University College of London, as well as a member of the Harvard Working Group for Sustainable Cities. In the following viewpoint, Duff argues that despite regulatory and zoning challenges that large-scale urban agriculture presents, it is ultimately inconceivable that city-dwellers should be wholly dependent upon massive corporations, some thousands of miles away, to provide them with food. Duff cites "energy and social capital" as major contributors to the increasing success of small- and medium-sized urban farming projects throughout cities in the United States and Europe, and he also cites Cuba's success as an example worth emulating. Duff acknowledges that industrial

Mike Duff, "How Cities Can Embrace Urban Agriculture and Weaken the Grip of 'Big Food,'" *The Global Urbanist*, August 25, 2010. Copyright © 2010. All rights reserved. Reproduced by permission.

agriculture will most likely remain part of the system that provides food to city-dwellers around the world, but he insists that eventually city planners must comply with the demands of members of the urban farming movement and include farmland in designs for cities.

As you read, consider the following questions:

1. Which countries are cited by the author as having seen success with planned urban farming?
2. What land use designation does Duff suggest for zoning and regulation in Detroit and other cities struggling with the issue of urban agriculture?
3. What kind of crop does Duff say will most likely have to be grown first before vegetable farming begins?

Honey from Hackney or Philadelphia, tomatoes from Brooklyn or Queens—on both sides of the Atlantic, growing one's own, and doing so locally, is becoming part of the zeitgeist. And with increasing media coverage of an impending food crisis it seems impossible to ignore.

City managers are increasingly looking for ways to understand it—both from a regulation perspective, but equally to determine what is needed to foster and support these activities.

The rationale for supporting agriculture within cities isn't immediately obvious—it isn't prominent in modern cities, nor has it ever really been typical, to have food production within urban areas. In many ways, being surrounded by agricultural fields was always a sign that one had ventured outside the city limits—it was a defining non-urban factor.

Urban Farming Does Exist

Allotments in England, *Schrebergarten* in Germany, *Organopónicos* in Cuba, [and] community gardens in the US are all planner-recognised urban agricultural land uses and illustrate that food production in cities is not unheard of. It would seem that as long as urban food remains within a small-to-medium physical scale, and essentially non-commercial (or at least "social" in its degree of commerciality), it can successfully pass within current urban regulations. For the most part, these current methods of deploying agriculture within cities imply that it plays a complementary or additional role to other food sources such as grocery stores and markets, and that it makes efficient use of small parcels of land without being land-hungry.

Essentially, urban agriculture is non-threatening to the status quo in its current formats. It is generally argued that it is incapable of producing food at costs which compete with 'big food' (or industrial food). Research is now showing, however, that the elimination of transport costs through local growing, and the design of rooftop greenhouses that are parasitic (*i.e.*, that harvest waste energy from their host buildings) such as the Bronx tomatoes to be grown this year [2010], can bring this produce well within, and indeed under, supermarket prices.

And what is to say that a little scale is not what is lacking to bring locally-grown urban produce within the supermarket price point? The Cuban *Organopónicos* also offer an (admittedly non-capitalist) model which has proven affordable to thousands.

It is interesting therefore to see an example of an American city, at the centre of a complicated battle over urban agriculture. Detroit, a city formerly known for its auto industry and musical heritage, and more recently for its suffering at the hands of our current recession and a crash in the car industry, is a hot bed of urban agriculture and 'urban ag'-related discussion at present.

As Motor City has been shrinking, more and more land has become available, either for free or at rock-bottom prices, and used by those residents who remain, as land for growing crops. Detroiters are a hardy bunch, and many who could leave the city still remain, and those who can't leave their financially underwater properties are often the voices and energy behind these proj-

Using Vacant City Land for Commercial Farming

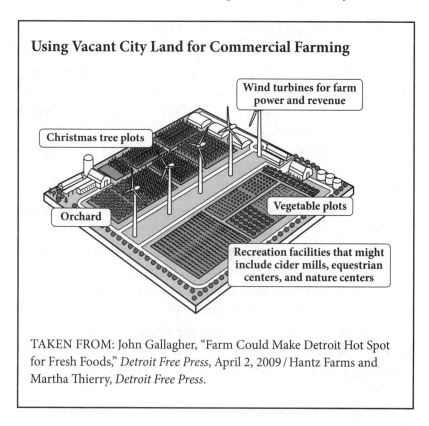

Wind turbines for farm power and revenue

Christmas tree plots

Orchard

Vegetable plots

Recreation facilities that might include cider mills, equestrian centers, and nature centers

TAKEN FROM: John Gallagher, "Farm Could Make Detroit Hot Spot for Fresh Foods," *Detroit Free Press*, April 2, 2009 / Hantz Farms and Martha Thierry, *Detroit Free Press*.

ects. At present there are almost 900 community garden projects across the city.

An interesting pastime, these are also a critical food-growing resource for a city where, increasingly, the 'big shed' food sellers have moved out as population densities wane, leaving the local liquor store one of the only places to buy food—if you can call it that.

Accommodating Urban Agriculture

While on the one side, these urban agricultural projects are finding favour and support with the city, for their economic, aesthetic, social, educational, health and open-space related benefits, the city is also faced with a number of dilemmas.

Most importantly, how to regulate them? As more and more land becomes available, and prices continue to languish, larger urban agricultural projects become more viable. Is there a limit to how big one of these projects can be? Are there regulations regarding what can be practised on the site—can one keep cows, chickens, bees, horses, for example? Is an abattoir [slaughterhouse] urban agriculture? Or a battery farm? The City of Detroit is confronted with a need to develop a strategy regarding these issues.

At the same time, machinations regarding the State's 'Right to Farm Act' have the city worried that if they begin to redesignate land within the city limits as 'agricultural' their influence over these tracts will be diluted, and their fiscal entitlement to tax the land may be at risk. It may also open up the land to agricultural uses which are anti-urban, either in scale or other impacts. It seems that a hybrid land use designation called 'urban agricultural uses' is what is required here—one which thinks about urban food production across the myriad sectors in which it operates.

While this debate rumbles on, a certain John Hantz pushes ahead on the Hantz Farm project, with his own money. Hantz seeks to buy up substantial tracts of land at current market prices, to take his large scale projects forward. Hantz's project, from some imagery, is reminiscent of Dickson Despommier's Vertical Farm research being undertaken at Columbia University, deployed at an urban scale.

A Grey Regulatory Environment

But it is important to note that it is being taken forward in the aforementioned grey regulatory environment. While the project will create jobs, and will bring dollars to a city in dire need of them, it might not, at least initially, bring the kind of agriculture that Detroiters expect. It is anticipated that most of the first few years of growth will be 'forestry products'—Christmas trees, that is, and the byproducts which can be made and sold from these pine trees. Not surprisingly, the ideological conflict between those behind the community garden movement, and these larger, more commercial operations attempting to literally gain ground in Detroit, rages.

It often feels that our modern cities, and even our modern urban sustainability work, leaves food production by the wayside. We are grateful to 'big shed' food retailers for feeding us, and are therefore somewhat comfortable with the likes of Tesco [a United Kingdom supermarket chain] for example, having the largest property portfolio in the United Kingdom, capable of holding city planning authorities to ransom.

It must be said, though, that despite the economic barriers created by big supermarkets and the industrial food chain which supports them, urban agriculture is clearly happily flourishing at the small to medium scale. Increasingly, as the business modelling work behind the New York schemes show (the Bronx and Columbia University examples above), it is becoming possible to compete with big food, producing organic, transport-free, cross-seasonal produce, within the most urban of places. So much adversity has done the urban agricultural movement well, it would seem, as it has given it lofty ambition. It is now that the interesting bit must happen—the success of such products will inevitably push these projects to upscale, and cities must be ready, and accommodating.

The energy and social capital behind such projects, which is increasingly 'movement-esque', is an incredible asset which even the most top-down of city legislators must acknowledge is worth supporting. Detroit is a fantastic example—where Mayor Bing has employed a team of designers (including my company) to 're-imagine' the city, in part, by auditing the bottom-up initiatives underway there, and bringing these together, into the city's future planning, by contributing strategic direction. Detroit acknowledges that it needs to get ready to accommodate urban agriculture at a larger scale.

Engaging Urbanites in Shaping Cities

Food, and therefore urban agriculture, is a particularly powerful tool to get urbanites engaged in shaping their cities. For a
start, it is common to everyone—we all eat. On top of that, it is
social—we socialise our children around the dinner table, celebrate achievements over nice meals, feel good, worse, bad or better from eating; it is *economic*—we spend our cash on food, and
its growth, processing, delivery marketing and retailing creates
jobs, and it is 'big business'; and it is *environmental*—it shapes
our landscapes, organises our open spaces, forms habitats, provides ecosystem services, shapes our cities, [and] creates and ab-
sorbs pollution whilst demanding and supplying resources.

Seen like this, food can not only be a lens into how we live,
but a way for those involved in it to shape our inhabitation directly. The usurpation of the majority of our food chains by 'big
food'—companies like Monsanto, who patent seeds and force
farmers to buy new each year; Cargill, whose stranglehold with
three other companies on US grain markets means they almost
set prices; and Tesco, whose retained large bank could accommodate 145 more mega-stores and gives them leverage over city
planners—suddenly seems ludicrous, if not dangerous.

Why should these companies stand between citizens, and
their right to shape their cities and lives? If we choose to break
bread with our neighbours, why should an essentially social
transaction line the pockets of these companies? The truth of
the matter is, they are so big, in numbers, in assets and in geo-
graphic scale, they are almost beyond control. They are certainly
beyond the reaches of city-level legislators. It would appear we
have quietly stood by as one of our fundamental human needs
has become an energy-intensive, polluting and unhealthy cash
cow, delivering profits to a select few.

While it must be said that a sustainable food system, for a
growing population will be diverse in sourcing, and therefore include 'big food', the environmental, social and economic impact
of this industrial food chain must mean that they cannot be our

sole provider. We would not, as city designers, have developed city road networks without petrol stations to fuel our vehicles— why is it that we think it is sensible to have cities which don't produce fuel for our people? It is not!

"Given the social, environmental and economic returns that urban food systems can deliver, we should find ways to nurture them to grow."

The Best Business Model for Urban Agriculture Has Yet to Be Determined

Cheryl Kollin

Cheryl Kollin has a master's of business administration degree in sustainable business from the Bainbridge Graduate Institute and works as a social enterprise consultant to nonprofit groups. She also works with a community garden and food donation program. In the following viewpoint, Kollin maintains that innovation and customized service are two keys to success in urban farming, but access to land and determining how large a farm must be to achieve profitability remain problems. According to Kollin, former professional basketball player Will Allen's Growing Power project is an example of urban agriculture innovation, with its large-scale compost operation, fish tanks, and youth skills programs, which feed ten thousand low-income residents of the Milwaukee area and provide numerous other social services to the community. Market specialization is another business model advocated by Kollin, taking into account the particular demographic groups—such as im-

migrants—in any given community so that those groups can be offered the kinds of produce most use in their cooking and also so that they might gain valuable business experience to ensure their continued financial success.

As you read, consider the following questions:

1. According to Kollin, what is the "social return on invest-ment" that urban farms such as Will Allen's gain?
2. According to the author, what are some options the "agri-preneurs" have once they graduate from the Offshoots Farm program?
3. How does Glynn Lloyd describe the advantages of farm franchising, as described by Kollin?

Urban farming may sound like an oxymoron, but judging from the 375-person sell-out crowd at the first Urban Farm Summit in Washington, D.C., the idea is catching on like organics at Walmart.

The recent one-day event, called Sowing Seeds Here and Now, was organized by Engaged Community Offshoots (ECO), a fledgling non-profit urban farm based just outside D.C. in Prince George's County, Maryland. The summit agenda spotlighted the reasons why urban farms are sprouting up all over: They increase food security by growing food locally. They give under-served urban neighborhoods access to fresh foods. They strengthen lo-cal economies by keeping dollars circulating within the commu-nity. They engage consumers, who learn how food is grown. They reduce 'food miles' and fossil fuel use. And they create jobs.

Urban farms are growing more than food. They are growing community.

A New Business Model

As a social enterprise consultant, I'm fascinated to watch new business models emerge. Nascent urban farmers are not only literally breaking new ground, but they are finding they enjoy competitive advantages over their rural counterparts. Buyers will pay a premium for custom-grown vegetables that can be picked and delivered the same day.

"I can walk in to a restaurant with a seed catalog and ask the chef what varieties of lettuce, zucchini, or beets he'd like me to grow, just for his menu," explains Vinnie Bevivino, director of Urban Farming Operations at ECO. "He can also tell me when he wants delivery and I'll synchronize my planting schedule with his seasonal menus. He won't get that kind of customized service from a national produce chain."

Yet to make their business work, urban farmers must contend with two challenges that rural farmers typically don't face—accessing land and scaling operations large enough to be profitable. Urban land suitable for farming is expensive and, even when land is available it comes in smaller lot-sized parcels rather than in acres. Urban land is at such a premium that farmers have to get creative and grow more densely to make their business viable.

Innovators are finding a way to make urban farming work. Will Allen, the guru of urban farming and the creator of Growing Power in Milwaukee, has been able to grow enough food in 14 greenhouses sited on two acres of land in the middle of a food desert to feed 10,000 local residents. The non-profit turns millions of tons of food waste into compost to grow vegetables, and to feed Tilapia and Lake Perch in tanks. But even more impressive is Growing Power's social return on investment: They include engaging youth in work readiness, life skills, construction techniques, and writing skills; employing convicts for summer work; reducing crime in the neighborhood; and teaching adults from all over the world hands-on urban farming.

To spread urban farming, Growing Power offers an eight month training course. The Washington-based ECO staff, after completing it, is beginning to replicate such holistic practices as hoop houses (inexpensive structures made from curved tubular metal frame and covered with greenhouse plastic sheeting to grow food year round), rain catchment and drip irrigation systems for efficient watering, solar panels and anaerobic digesters that make electricity from waste. They're also starting closed-loop aquaculture, where plants filter waste from fish, and vermiculture, raising worms that turn food waste into nutrient-rich compost.

A Customized Business Model

While operations can be replicated, ECO must figure out its own business model, tailored for its community's needs, growing conditions and consumer market. ECO incorporated as a non-profit just six months ago [in spring 2010]. With grants and in-kind corporate support, the group has secured permission to use county land just over the Washington, D.C., border.

Vinnie explains how they make use of two small parcels: We devote two acres just to make compost, turning 10 tons of food waste donated by Whole Foods and 30 cubic yards of wood chips donated by Pepco, our local utility company, into 40 cubic yards of compost, which we will sell as well as use on our own farm. On another half acre, we grow high-quality produce, fish and bee products to sell to local residents at farmers markets, food coops, restaurants, and public schools.

ECO just launched its Offshoots Farm Network. "The network is a group of interrelated agricultural enterprises established to train and employ our underserved community members to produce food for ourselves," explains Christopher Washington, ECO's Director of Business Operations. With a Kellogg Foundation grant secured by Crossroads Farmer's Market, a farmer's market located in Takoma Park, Maryland, ECO and the Offshoots Farm Network collaborate to help immigrant farmers. "We call this new generation of farmers 'agripreneurs'", says Christopher. The initial class of five is comprised of immigrants from Ethiopia and Latin American countries who were farmers in their home countries. Rose Sesero, one of the students, explains why she entered the training program, "I am a hard working person, a fast learner and I would like to make a difference in my life. Also, I would like to help people to change their diet, by focusing on increasing vegetable consumption and having less meat. Back in Ethiopia I grew flowers as a hobby."

Some students come with college degrees but may not speak English yet. They will learn how to navigate the business of farming in our society—by writing a business plan, selling at farmers markets, and learning how to transact with SNAP and WIC (food stamps) forms of payment.

"Once they graduate, the agripreneurs can decide where they fit into the local food value chain. They might choose to continue working on ECO's farm, or they could grow their own produce and sell it under the ECO brand label, or they might choose to strike out on their own," Christopher says. "Whatever they do, we want to remain supportive."

Franchising Urban Agriculture

Elsewhere, other models are being tested. Glynn Lloyd's City Growers, LLC is an urban farm franchise business that Lloyd started in his home town of Roxbury, Massachusetts. "I wanted to address the interconnected issues of health, obesity, green jobs, and economic development," he says. Last year [in 2009], Glynn looked around his neighborhood and shook his head. "I saw a lot of vacant land, a lot of unemployed people, and an unmet demand for locally-grown food," he recalls.

Glynn's idea is to create a turn-key operation—but instead of a fast food chain, he is investing in training residents as farmers and turning vacant lots into urban farms. He's improving the soil and installing hoop houses, irrigation, and fencing. By creating an urban farm social franchise, Glynn believes he can eventually generate $60,000 per acre in revenue while creating jobs and giving local control to the resident farmers. As a franchise, City Growers would take care of marketing, branding, sales, and quality control. This frees the farmers to focus on, well, farming.

Glynn's other business City Fresh Foods, Inc., which he started with his brother Sheldon 15 years ago provides a ready market for processing the fresh produce and turning it into meals for Boston's public schools, vertically integrating at least part of the local food system.

Glynn only launched City Growers this spring [2010]. He estimates that there are 800 acres of vacant land in the Boston area, but admits he's facing hurdles around land acquisition. "On land owned by non-profits, we have to build consensus for using land as a farm. On private land, we have to challenge the current zoning laws that don't allow farms, and on public land, officials are hesitant to encumber land that has development potential when eventually the economy improves," Glynn says. City Growers started with one-quarter of an acre of non-profit land in the middle of a Dorchester neighborhood and another 1-1/2 acres of land owned by private landowners in a neighboring town. Even though City Growers is a for-profit, the business has recently partnered with New Ecology, a non-profit to generate funding to support their social mission.

It's much too early to tell which might prove the better business model for urban farming—ECO's Agripreneurs or City Grower's franchise. Some critics believe that urban farms won't be viable in the long term if they depend on grants. Even Milwaukee-based Growing Power isn't economically sustainable; it received $1 million in grants over the last five years to support its 40 full time and 40 part time staff, and it relies on 3,000 volunteers. Others say urban farms will never support a community's food demand.

And yet re-localizing even part of our food system is about much more than providing food. How do we value creating more jobs, providing more fresh fruits and vegetables to underserved communities and reconnecting people more viscerally with their food? Glynn quotes Jared Diamond, the author of *Collapse*, who has written: "The rise and fall of a society starts with its food system."

Cities may not need urban farms to survive. But given the social, environmental and economic returns that urban food systems can deliver, we should find ways to nurture them to grow.

Periodical and Internet Sources Bibliography

The following articles have been selected to supplement the diverse views presented in this chapter.

Mark Edward Lee	"Urban Agriculture and the Green-Collar Citizen," *Catalysts for Intellectual Capital 2020—Leadership Institute,* 2009. www.leadershipinstitute.org.
John Mogk and Sarah Kwiatkowski	"Urban Farming Should Take Root Here," *Crain's Detroit Business,* April 18, 2010.
Chuck Plunkett	"Denver Mayoral Candidate Hancock Promotes Urban Gardens as Economic Engine," *Denver Post,* May 27, 2011.
The Plus (blog)	"Urban Farms Represent Economic Opportunity," May 2, 2011. www.theplus.us.
Emmaline Pohnl	"Finding Farmville: Inner-City Farms Transform Urban Neighborhoods with Jobs and Fresh Food," *Daily Northwestern,* February 22, 2011.
Sara Prendergast	"Community Gardens and Urban Agriculture: Reclaiming the Marketplace," California Polytechnic State University, Spring 2010. http://digital commons.calpoly.edu.
Charles Redell	"Down (Town) on the Farm," Sustainable Industries, September 1, 2010. www.sustainableindus tries.com.
Emily Wilkins	"Growing Prosperity," *State News,* May 24, 2010.
Matthew Yglesias	"We Could Subsidize Urban Farming, but We Probably Shouldn't," ThinkProgress, July 6, 2009. www.thinkprogress.org.

CHAPTER 3

How Does Urban Agriculture Affect Particular Groups?

Chapter Preface

Every year tens of thousands of people seek refugee status in the United States, due to persecution or the threat of persecution in their home countries. Typically the people who come to the United States as refugees first leave their own countries—often with few or no personal items and frequently to save their lives—and go to a neighboring country, where they end up in overcrowded, sometimes dangerous, refugee camps, where they may be forced to live for years before their applications for refugee status are approved by the US government. Once in the United States, they usually receive help from refugee resettlement agencies and often end up living in urban housing among immigrants from the same or different countries. Refugees rarely have English language skills, and many come from rural backgrounds. Additionally, they are faced with an unfamiliar culture and foods, which can add to the disorientation of the experience. Furthermore, while refugee men sometimes manage to find work at jobs that do not require fluency in English, women have a much harder time because in many cases they must remain at home to care for children, leaving the women alienated and slowing their successful assimilation into their new communities.

Enter urban farming. In 2006 Rachel Bonar, who was then serving as director of the women's program at Catholic Charities of Northeast Kansas in Kansas City, discovered that the women in her group missed having land to farm as they had in their native countries of Sudan, Burundi, Somalia, Bhutan, and Burma (Myanmar). In response, the agency gave them a space to garden by its offices. The garden was so abundant that the following year Catholic Charities teamed up with the Kansas City Center for Urban Agriculture to develop New Roots for Refugees Farm, which includes a Farm Business Development Program, where the women spend winters learning English through the study of the agriculture business. When they are ready to move forward with the business aspect of the farm, they organize their own Community Supported Agriculture (CSA) shares throughout the greater Kansas City community.

Meanwhile, in West Valley City, Utah, a similar venture between Salt Lake County, the Utah Refugee Coalition, and the International Rescue Committee, broke ground for a one-and-a-half-acre farm that will be broken up into smaller plots as well as "micro farms" to give refugees experience in planning, growing, and marketing their produce to customers in addition to teaching them English. The largest such program was spearheaded by the US Department of Health and Human Services' Office of Refugee Resettlement. Nineteen urban agriculture programs in cities around the United States were awarded grants to partner with various refugee service organizations, including the International Institute of St. Louis, in Missouri, which has eleven refugees going through the first three-year program. Like the programs in other cities, English and business farming classes are at the fore. The viewpoints in the following chapter discuss how farming in a city environment affects different groups of people.

> "African Americans have been slow
> to get involved in the urban farming
> movement. . . . Among them, young
> adults . . . seem the most reluctant."

Young African Americans
Are Ambivalent About
Urban Agriculture

Krishna Ramanujan

Krishna Ramanujan is a science writer for Cornell University. In the following viewpoint, Ramanujan discusses the possible reasons why young black urbanites seem ambivalent about getting involved in urban farming despite the fact that their communities would, in many cases, benefit most from such projects. According to the author, some black Americans may associate farming with southern blacks after the Civil War, who were forced to make a meager living by sharecropping, a system in which usually white landowners allowed usually black farmers to use parcels of land in exchange for a portion (or share) of their yield. While many older blacks may have fond memories of gardening with their older relatives, says Ramanujan, younger generations have only impressions of poverty, injustice, and servitude. Furthermore, Ramanujan adds, time and transportation figure prominently for lower-income blacks, as many are simply unable to take time away from much-needed employment and have no viable means of transportation to and from urban farms.

As you read, consider the following questions:
1. How do children influence their parents' buying and eating habits, according to the author?
2. According to Ramanujan, what illnesses are African American more prone to than other groups?
3. Which US government agency used discriminatory practices against black farmers, according to the author?

Over the last decade, urban gardens have cropped up in every major U.S. city like little flowers in cracked asphalt. New York City's five boroughs, for example, now contain more than 600 urban farms. As a result, some people call urban agriculture a food revolution—it offers a form of self-determination for people to grow their own food in lower-income minority neighborhoods that often lack access to fresh produce.

But the movement's greatest success may come by changing people's relationships to food. Nowhere is this trend more apparent than in school gardens. A recent University of California–Berkeley study found that young children who gardened and learned about nutrition ate one-and-a-half more servings of fruits and vegetables per day than those who did not.

In Detroit, meanwhile, 60 school gardens are now linked with the Detroit Public School system. Thanks to their gardening experience, "children are influencing the purchasing power of their parents" by pointing out the healthier food options they learned about, said Monica White, a sociologist at Wayne State University who studies urban farming in Detroit.

Urban Blacks Lack Healthy Food

Why is that important? Well, consider that the entire city of Detroit, which is 80 percent African American, has no major supermarkets. Across the country, the rise of American automobile culture, white flight to the suburbs, the big box supermarket model, and structural racism are all to blame for the same stark pattern in poor minority inner city neighborhoods where there are few, distant grocery stores but plentiful liquor stores, corner markets, and fast food restaurants. At the same time, a lack of healthy food choices is strongly correlated to higher rates of dietary-related illnesses like diabetes, hypertension, heart disease, and obesity. All of these health concerns are greatest for African Americans compared to other groups.

Given these issues, urban agriculture promises a lot: Fresh vegetables in so-called 'food deserts,' job training, employment, information about nutrition, cooking classes, and self-reliance in the face of a biased food system.

But with notable exceptions, African Americans have been slow to get involved, in spite of a long and rich agricultural tradition in the South. Among them, young adults, who may have the most time and energy, seem the most reluctant.

"When I talk to black folks about growing food, the younger ones do have a lot of resistance," said Nikki Henderson. She serves as executive director of People's Grocery, a non-profit that grows and distributes fresh food and offers job training, nutrition and cooking classes, and community events to residents of West Oakland, which is a low-income, mostly minority neighborhood with no grocery stores. "But for the folks that have memories of their grandmothers' gardens there is a spark of recognition," she added.

Mixed Reactions

White said she's also seen reactions from African Americans to urban agriculture that range from enthusiasm to outright dismissal. The sociologist is also on the board of directors for the Detroit Black Community Food Security Network, which runs a two-acre model city farm and recently developed a food access policy that was adopted by the Detroit city council.

Toward a Unified Movement

While I agree that participants of the progressive food move-ment need to recognize and be aware of their privileges and differences when they enter a disadvantaged community to work, I also don't think the answer is to split the movement and make white or "privileged" farmers and activists feel their help is unwanted by the minority and low-income communi-ties they are working in.

Natasha Bowens, "Food Justice: It's
Not Black and White in Detroit," Grist,
November 18, 2010.

"You have to look at it by generation," she said. While African Americans in their 60s and older embrace farming and garden-ing, those in their 40s have more mixed reactions; and African Americans in their 20s and 30s may have the least connection to agriculture. "We haven't found a way to make gardening and farming cool," White said. "We need more artists to talk about it, to make it hip."

Furthermore, discrimination over the last century has re-duced familial ties to farming and knowledge about growing food. Many African American–owned farms were lost in part due to half a century of discriminatory practices by the USDA [US Department of Agriculture], which unjustly denied farm loans or subjected African American farmers to longer waits for loan approvals than white applicants. In 1920, for example, one in seven U.S. farms were operated by African Americans; by 1992, the number had fallen to one in 100. A lawsuit by black farmers and two settlements (in 1999 and 2010) were reached with the USDA for a total of $2.25 billion, much of which has yet to be paid.

Also, detachment from agriculture may relate to cultural issues that followed slavery, said Henderson. "We come from a history of slaves on plantations and growing food against our will," she said. African Americans who moved north sought a new more affluent and sophisticated life that distanced them from slavery, southern agricultural roots, and appearing 'country,' said Henderson. The vestiges of such stigmas may turn some away from urban farming today.

Time Is a Factor for the Poor

Gardening can be a tough sell for those struggling with chronic poverty, said Jemila Sequeira, a community organizer in Ithaca, New York. She co-leads Gardens 4 Humanity, a grassroots program that raises awareness about nutrition and builds garden spaces in lower-income and African-American areas near schools and subsidized housing around Ithaca. The white, rural impoverished people near the city are a little more receptive to gardening, said Sequeira, "because they don't have the historical backdrop," and they may have more access to land. But many low-income people interested in gardening and eating better often lack time and transportation, even when plots are provided, as with Gardens 4 Humanity.

"It's hard for people to hear what they need to eat to be healthier, especially when they don't have systems in place to meet those needs," she added. Sequeira said that showing compassion and being a woman of color from a working class background helps her both relate to and gain trust from the people she serves. For these reasons, urban gardening would benefit from more African American leaders at the local level. In Ithaca, "there are only a few [African Americans] out there in the community in positions of leadership with resources to reach people," Sequeira added.

In order to engage the local community, Gardens 4 Humanity invites a broad range of people to install raised garden beds in key locations. The People's Grocery and the Detroit Black

Community Food Security Network also host events at community garden spaces, where urban farmers use the opportunity to teach gardening. At a recent such 'grub party' in West Oakland, People's Grocery offered free food, childcare, information about gardening and raising chickens, and a goat milking demonstration. "It was shocking how many African American folk from the hood were excited about milking the goats," said Henderson.

With such events, farmer's markets and food distribution services, food activists are making some inroads. "I think produce is becoming more available in those places that are most food insecure," said White, referring to those communities where economic and physical barriers prevent access to healthy food.

At the same time, the future of this movement and greater involvement from African Americans may gain momentum from the next generation. Josh Dolan, who co-leads Gardens 4 Humanity with Sequeira, manages the project's youth and children's gardens and has organized new gardens at two schools in Ithaca. "We try to catch kids while they are young, by providing spaces in neighborhoods to grow vegetables that we teach them about," Dolan said. The strategy may have far-reaching effects.

With children, White added, "there's an avenue, a point of entry."

"*Urban farming among Latino immigrants passes down history from the homeland while keeping families healthy.*"

Latino Americans Reconnect with Their Heritage Through Urban Agriculture

Brenda Becerra

Brenda Becerra is an activist associated with the Little Village Environmental Justice Organization in Chicago, Illinois. In the following viewpoint, Becerra finds that Latinos in the United States have been drawn to the urban agriculture movement because so many came from farming families in their native countries. According to Becerra, community and school gardening has increased over the past few years, with associated education programs serving to make Latinos—who suffer from many of the same chronic health problems that blacks do—more aware of the health benefits of a better diet. Additionally, Becerra notes, agriculture programs in Latino communities tend to focus on reducing food expenditures through gardening, as well as the social interaction that comes from such projects. Contrasted with African Americans, who may view farming as a symbol of past institutional racism,

Becerra asserts, Latino heritage is strongly connected to farming, with detachment from the land considered a great loss of identity and a form of oppression.

As you read, consider the following questions:

1. According to the author, how many Americans and how many American children in low-income communities live more than a mile away from a supermarket?
2. What is the "mission" of the group Roots and Rays, as related by Becerra?
3. In what ways might losing touch with the land be a form of oppression for Latinos, according to the author?

Xochitl Sandoval, 19, keeps her Mexican culture alive. When Sandoval gardens, she feels a connection that gives her pride.

"When my grandparents come to visit from México, they complain about the boredom they feel because there is nothing to do except sit and watch television. They are used to getting up at sunrise and tending to their crops and their animals," said Sandoval. "This urban setting depresses them. Even my dad, who has been in the U.S. for years, already eases some of his frustration when I ask him to take a look at my garden or when I ask if a certain food is ready to be eaten."

"It seems like urban agriculture is the best option I have if I want to eat healthy food. In these times, it seems like my biggest worry should be what I eat. The list of ingredients used to make a simple orange juice is becoming more extensive and is including more words that I don't know and can't pronounce," said Sandoval. "It really makes me feel good to know that I can grow traditional vegetables and fruits in the city, in my backyard, and that I know that these vegetables and fruits will be composted and deposited back into my yard."

Due to the traditional diet and lack of fresh produce in communities, Latinos' risk of having Type 2 diabetes is almost twice that of non-Hispanic whites in the U.S. According to a USDA [US Department of Agriculture] survey, about 23.5 million Americans, including 6.5 million children, live in low-income areas that are more than a mile away from a supermarket.

According to 2009 statistics from the American Heart Association, 39.6 percent of Latinos are overweight and 27.5 percent are obese. Among Mexican American children ages 2–19, 40.8 percent of males and 35.0 percent of females are both overweight and obese. Among Mexican American children ages 2–19, 23.2 percent of males and 18.5 percent of females are obese.

A Cultural Connection

Urban farming among Latino immigrants passes down history from the homeland while keeping families healthy. In the past few years, there has been an increase in urban farming and community gardens in Latino communities [in Chicago] such as Little Village and Pilsen. There are open spaces that include vegetable gardens, flower gardens, school gardens, community gardens, natural areas and urban farms.

The Little Village Environmental Justice Organization (LVEJO) is a non-profit organization that works with the people to make the community a better living environment for everyone.

LVEJO has planted three community gardens, including one located between Joseph E. Gary and Josefa Ortiz de Dominguez schools. The school garden was designed as a collaboration of 6th-grade students and Green Corps, a program for college graduates that provides them with an academic grounding in their field choice and gives them experience working with organizations they are interested in. The garden gives children and adults a chance to learn together in an intergenerational exchange of knowledge. It teaches children to be sustainable at an early age. LVEJO has also done over 200 home gardens with the permission of homeowners who offer their front lawn or back yard to the community.

The Urban Agriculture campaign at LVEJO launched a Spring Committee that is working on growing backyard and community gardens throughout Little Village. One of their community gardens is located at Amor de Dios United Methodist Church at 2356 South Sawyer Avenue. The Amor de Dios community garden provides fresh produce for their food pantry, which serves 600 families twice a week.

Community Gardens in Food Deserts

Many Latino communities only have options to fatty foods and not enough of healthy foods. Districts with little or no access to healthy foods are what are called food deserts. Carolina Macias, one of the founding members of the community garden at Amor de Dios Church, said that some of her friends have to take two buses to get to the closest Whole Foods or Trader Joe's. The trip takes them more than an hour just to get access to fresh produce.

Amairani Galvan, LVEJO Urban Agriculture campaign volunteer, has seen the number of community gardens increase in the community. Her first experience with urban agriculture was when she helped her grandparents maintain their backyard garden as a child. Now she is in process of learning how to harvest. "A sustainable community is very important," said Galvan. "It is important for Latino immigrants to practice urban agriculture because a lot of us come from agricultural backgrounds. This way we can show what work we can do and how far we can go with it." Galvan hopes to pass down her knowledge and maybe have a farm of her own one day.

The Pilsen community is working towards a greener community. Residents search for any vacant lot that they can find to turn into a beautiful garden from which the whole community can enjoy. Pilsen now has at least 5 community gardens: Roots and Rays, Growing Station, El Jardin de las Mariposas

Success Based on Trust

At its base, the Local Food Revolution is based on a system of trust. Trust in nature's rules. Trust in our neighbor's integrity. Trust in our community's ability to meet the growing challenges of re-localization in a time of global collapse. Trust in the health of food grown using organic and permaculture practices.

Michael Brownlee of Transition Boulder says, "Community will be the most important natural resource of the 21st Century." All community depends on the ability of people to trust each other and the process of economic survival they engage in.

Public policy must regenerate trust in our agricultural and food systems. The goal is a renewed, reborn, regenerated trust that reconnects us to each other and to the land that sustains us. "Local food you can trust."

Christopher Bedford, "Public Policy,"
Feeding the Roots, Wallace Global Fund,
January 2009.

(The Butterfly Garden), Xochiquetzal Peace Garden and Orozco School Garden. Together, they form the newly founded Pilsen Green Alliance.

When Claire Mitchell, founding member of Roots and Rays, moved to Pilsen in 2007, she noticed a grassy vacant lot. In the summer of 2008, she started a perennial flower garden and small container garden where she grew vegetables and herbs. That once vacant lot has now become the Roots and Rays Community Garden located at the corner of Cullerton and Laflin.

Currently, the Roots and Rays garden has seven raised beds. They are growing edible vegetables and herbs. The crop includes three kinds of kale, collards, rainbow chard, mustard, tomatoes and cherry tomatoes, banana and bell peppers, carrots, radish, eggplant, zucchini, squash and watermelons. They are growing herbs from lemon basil, chives and thyme to oregano, sage and cilantro. The garden also includes a variety of ornamental flowers, a small pumpkin patch, and a decorative bed of "three sisters": corn, summer squash and beans.

Uniting the Community

Roots and Rays's mission is to provide education and awareness about the need for local sustainable food systems, provide healthy organic produce for the community and to provide a safe, green space in an otherwise environmentally unsound area.

"We believe community gardens are important in order to bring the community together, encourage peaceful social interaction and to demonstrate to the community's youth that a small group of dedicated and concerned individuals really can make a difference," said Christine Ferriter, [a] Roots and Rays trainee.

"Community gardening is a great way to demonstrate that it is not only easy, fun and nutritious to grow our own food but that kitchen gardens can also reduce family food budgets, conserve resources, and create opportunities for social and family interaction."

On a regular basis, they have youth groups coming from Casa Juan Diego and the Pilsen Wellness Center to learn about and take part in gardening. "We hope that these activities have nurtured an awareness of the environment and a sense of responsibility to the community in the young participants," said Ferriter.

"It's important for all people of color, not just Latino immigrants, to continue our legacy of agriculture because we have historically been connected to the soil. Through years of oppression we have slowly been detached from that connection," said Macias. "This connection, love and appreciation for the land are perhaps all we have left from our ancestors."

VIEWPOINT 3

| "Food sovereignty is best guaranteed
when food production is 'in women's
hands,' in the sense that women have
the means to control how food is
produced and consumed."

Urban Agriculture Represents
a Women's Political Movement

Silvia Federici, as told to Max Haiven

*Silvia Federici is a feminist scholar and emerita professor at Hofstra
University. Max Haiven is a postdoctoral fellow in the Department
of Art and Public Policy at New York University's Tisch School of
the Arts and an adjunct professor at the Division of Historical and
Critical Studies at the Nova Scotia College of Art and Design in
Halifax, Nova Scotia.* In the following viewpoint, Haiven interviews
Federici, who argues that prior to the rise of capitalism, women
were deeply engaged in agriculture, owned land, and were able to
have their own economy. With both colonialism and the market
economy, women lost their land rights and their control over food
production, according to Federici. Even poor women in developing countries who do subsistence farming to feed their families are
empowered by it, Federici asserts, and the fact that there is a renewed interest in and respect for agriculture in Western countries,
in the form of urban agriculture and the food justice movement,*

Max Haiven and Silvia Federici, "Silvia Federici, On Capitalism, Colonialism, Women, and
Food Politics," *Politics and Culture*, November 3, 2009. All rights reserved. Reproduced by
permission.

will, Federici asserts, allow communities, and especially women, to become more self-sufficient and less exploited as laborers. Federici cites movements in Latin America and Africa that demand that women be granted legal access to land for farming and the politicization of urban agriculture in the United States that indicate an increasing awareness of women's roles in attaining food sovereignty and food justice around the world.

As you read, consider the following questions:

1. At what point in European history did the division of labor in agriculture change, according to Federici?
2. About how many people worldwide does Federici estimate are employed in agricultural work?
3. According to the authors, what percentage of food is produced and consumed by women?

*M*ax Haiven for Politics and Culture: Your historical work has focused on the way the process of what [Karl] Marx called "primitive accumulation"—the way capitalism is created out of the destruction of other ways of life—has relied upon the systematic destruction of women's power and the "accumulation of divisions" amongst the working class. Can you speak to how this relates to the history of food politics?*

Silvia Federici: There is a direct relation between the destruction of the social and economic power of women in the "transition to capitalism" and the politics of food in capitalist society.

In every part of the world, before the advent of capitalism, women played a major role in agricultural production. They had access to land, the use of its resources and control over the crops they cultivated, all of which guaranteed their autonomy and economic independence from men. In Africa, they had their farming and cropping systems, which were the source of a specific female culture, and they were in charge of the selection of seeds, an operation that was crucial to the prosperity of the community and whose knowledge was transmitted through the generations. The same was true of women's role in Asia and the Americas. In Europe as well, until the late medieval period, women had land-use rights and the use of the "commons"—woods, ponds, grazing grounds—that were an important source of sustenance. In addition to farming with men, they had their gardens where they cultivated vegetables as well as medicinal herbs and plants.

Both in Europe and the regions the Europeans colonized, primitive accumulation and capitalist development changed this situation. With land privatization and the expansion of monetary relations, a deeper division of labor developed in agriculture that separated food production for profit from food production for direct consumption, devalued reproductive work, starting from subsistence farming, and appointed men as the chief agricultural producers, whereas women were relegated to the rank of "helpers," field hands, or domestic workers.

In colonial Africa, for example, British and French officers systematically favored men with regard to allocations of land, equipment, and training, the mechanization of agriculture being the occasion for a further marginalization of women's agricultural activities. They also disrupted female farming by forcing women to assist their husbands in the cultivation of cash crops, thus altering the power relations between women and men and instigating new conflicts between them. To this day, the colonial system, whereby land titles are given only to men, continues to be the rule for "development agencies" and not in Africa alone.

It must be said that men have been accomplices in this process, not only claiming control over women's labor, but, in the face of growing land scarcity, conspiring to curtail women's communal land-use rights (wherever these survived) by rewriting the rules and conditions of belonging to the community.

Despite women's resistance to their marginalization, and their continuous engagement in subsistence farming and land reclamation struggles, these developments have had a profound effect on food production. As Vandana Shiva so powerfully described in her book *Staying Alive*, with the exclusion of women from access to land and the destruction of their control over food production, a large body of knowledge, practices, techniques that for centuries safeguarded the integrity of the land and the soil and the nutritional value of food has been lost.

Today, in the eyes of "development" agencies, the image of the female subsistence farmer is one of complete degradation. For example, this is how the latest World Bank annual report, dedicated to agriculture, begins: "an African woman bent under the sun, weeding sorghum in an arid field with a hoe, a child strapped on her back—a vivid image of rural poverty." For years in fact, following the footsteps of the Peruvian economist Hernando de Soto, the World Bank has tried to convince us that land is a dead asset when used for sustenance and shelter, and it becomes productive only when it is brought to a bank as collateral to gain credit. Behind this view is an arrogant philosophy that sees only money as creative of wealth, and believes capitalism and industry can recreate nature.

But the opposite is the case. With the demise of women's subsistence farming, an incredible wealth is increasingly being lost, with severe consequences for the quality and quantity of the food available to us. What the Bank does not tell us is that much of the nutritional value of food is lost through the industrialization of agriculture. It also does not tell us that it is thanks to women's struggles to continue to provide for their families' consumption, often farming on unused public or private land, that millions of people have been able to survive in the face of economic liberalization.

This all brings up the importance of agricultural labor, especially women's labour, to the processes of globalization. What's your sense of how agricultural labour fits into how we are conceptualizing global labour today? Numerically, it remains the biggest employer of people's time, especially women's time, worldwide. But it seems to fall off the radar in analyses of the changing forms of work and capital these days.

It is a mistake for left[ist] movements to underestimate, practically and analytically, the importance of agricultural work in today's political economy and, consequently, the transformative capacity of the struggles that farmers are making on this terrain. Certainly, the capitalists are not making this mistake. As the World Bank reports I mentioned (among other documents) indicate, the reorganization of agricultural relations always takes priority in its restructuring programs.

Although the number of people employed in agricultural work is impressive (probably amounting to two billion people), its importance is not to be measured only by its sheer size. Most important is the contribution agricultural work makes to social reproduction. As I mentioned, subsistence agriculture in particular, mostly done by women, enables millions to live who would otherwise have no means to purchase food on the market. Moreover, the revalorization, extension, and reintegration of agricultural labor into our lives are a must if we wish to construct a self-sufficient, non-exploitative society.

There are many political groups and movements, also in the industrialized North (eco-feminists above all), who recognize this need. It is also encouraging that, over the last two decades, we have seen the growth of urban garden movements, returning agricultural work to the heart of our industrial metropolises. But unfortunately, many in the left have not yet overcome the legacy of class struggle in the industrial era with its unique stresses on the factory and the industrial proletariat, as well as its belief in a technological road to liberation from capitalism.

For example, in [Antonio] Negri and [Michael] Hardt's *Multitude* we read that the peasantry is destined to disappear from the historical scene because of the increasing integration of science and technology in the organization of agricultural production and the dematerialization of labor. It is disturbing that

Prevalence of Food Insecurity, 2009

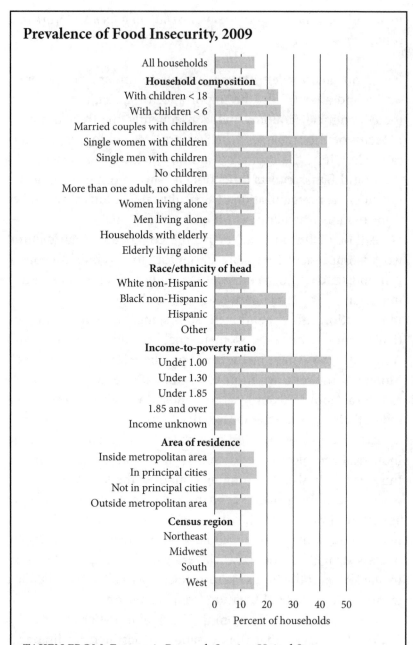

TAKEN FROM: Economic Research Service, United States Department of Agriculture, Current Population Survey Food Security Supplement, December 2009.

Negri and Hardt cite genetic engineering to support their view that the peasantry, as a historical category, is on its way to becoming defunct, given the fierce struggle farmers are conducting worldwide against genetically modified (GM) seeds, which, from this perspective, is already presumed defeated.

In reality, what we are witnessing is a process of re-peasantization and "rurbanization" which the present crisis can only accelerate. It's already occurring in China: former immigrants to the towns are returning to the rural areas destined to become a body of laborers in constant motion between these poles. In Africa too, many urban dwellers are now returning to the village, but they often move back and forth, because they cannot find sufficient means of survival in any single place. . . .

Your research on historical and contemporary women's labour and struggle has been extremely insightful. How do women's work and women's struggle factor into the politics of food sovereignty today?

Women's work and struggles are central to the question of "food sovereignty" today. Women are those who pay the highest price for the increase in food prices, and the fact that their access to land and capacity as agricultural producers have been severely undermined is one of the reasons why such price hikes are possible.

As I mentioned earlier, women have been the world's food producers and processors since time immemorial. To this day, in some parts of the world (Africa above all) 80% of the food consumed is produced by them. Their subsistence agriculture enables millions to live who could not otherwise purchase food on the market. However, their ability to grow food is increasingly threatened by increasing land scarcity, the privatization of land and water, the commercialization of agriculture, and the shift in most Third World countries to export-oriented agricultural production (now dubbed "high value" agriculture by the World Bank). These trends reinforce each other. To the extent that the land available to farmers is constantly diminishing, even in regions where the majority of the population depends on agriculture, women are subjected to exclusionary procedures by their male relatives and male members of their communities so that their access to land and customary rights are increasingly restricted. This represents a major threat to food production and the food consumption of large segments of the world population. It also places the control over the food consumed out of the hands of women.

A campaign is now taking place in Latin America and Africa, conducted by women's groups and associations who demand that women's rights to land be guaranteed in the laws and constitutions of their countries. Meanwhile, women have been at the forefront of urban farming and land struggles. In many African cities, from Accra to Kinshasa, they take over unused plots of land to grow maize, cassava, and peppers, changing the landscape of African towns, adding to their families' food and monetary budget, and boosting their own economic independence. But the battleground remains the redistribution of lands and the guarantee that women have full access to them and to the waters than run through them. As feminist writers like Maria Mies and Vandana Shiva have stressed, food sovereignty is best guaranteed when food production is "in women's hands," in the sense that women have the means to control how food is produced and consumed. . . .

While the global south has seen a huge rise in social movements contesting corporate globalization's sovereignty over food it seems that food movements in the global north, and especially in North America, have tended to follow a consumerist logic (slow food, eating organic, etc.). Do you think there are new political possibilities for organizing around food that move us beyond this?

The contrast is real, but a number of trends, in recent years, indicate that new ways of organizing around food are developing that move beyond the narrow concept of self-interest embodied in the demand for organic food.

First, there has been the urban gardens movement I mentioned before that has spread in several US cities. It has increasingly been acquiring a political dimension, thanks, in part, to the attacks against it by conservative politicians like former New York mayor Rudy Giuliani. His plan, to bulldoze dozens of gardens in New York in the mid '90s, raised everyone's consciousness and had the effect of turning gardening into a movement. We now realize that the gardens are the seeds of another economy, independent of the market. Not only do they fulfill an economic function by providing cheaper, fresher food that many could not otherwise afford, but they create a new sociality; they are places of gathering, cooperation, reciprocal education between people of different ages and cultures.

There is also a new interest, among youth in North America, for farming, for learning the properties of herbs and plants, and for creating a new relationship with nature. I continuously meet young people in the U.S. who are genuinely disgusted with the consumerist culture that surrounds them, and become vegetarian or vegan out of concern for the ecological and human cost of cattle raising as well as their refusal of animal suffering. The spread of food co-ops, Community Supported Agriculture, and groups such as Food Not Bombs, indicate the existence of this new consciousness.

The problem we face in building a mass movement is that changing consciousness is not enough to change food buying and eating practice. Lack of access to land, lack of money, space and time (to shop, cook, and learn about the conditions of production of what we eat) are the main obstacles in this respect. The food movement must be embedded in broader movements addressing the totality of our lives.

*"The real solution, of course, is jobs. . . .
As long as Detroit remains an
economic wasteland, its food problems
cannot be solved."*

The Urban Poor Need Supermarkets, Not Urban Agriculture

Richard Longworth

In the following viewpoint, Richard Longworth contends that cities with high rates of food insecurity need chain grocery stores rather than urban agriculture to lift their low-income residents out of the cycle of hunger. The end-products of urban farming, argues Longworth, are "niche" foods that only interest a wealthier, suburban market that can afford them and are generally not helpful to low-income urban dwellers. Longworth says that supporters of urban farming fail to understand the trend of farming in the United States. Chain supermarkets, says Longworth, offer affordable prices and quality products, yet they typically avoid poor urban areas, thus creating "food deserts." He cites the city of Detroit, which is known as one of the largest food deserts in the United States. As a solution, Longworth suggests city government forge a deal with retailing giant Wal-Mart to offer existing retail spaces rent-free in exchange for the promise of a long-term commitment and nutrition classes for residents. Richard Longworth is a senior fellow at the Chicago Council on Global Affairs.

As you read, consider the following questions:
1. From where does Longworth say most urban Detroiters came?
2. According to the author, what is the trend in farming in the United States?
3. What does Longworth suggest will make Wal-Mart's "savage personnel policies" more palatable to city government?

R esidents of Detroit are digging up vacant lots in their emptying city and turning them into urban farms. These little plots are an important source for produce for Detroiters for one big reason: there aren't many other sources.

Detroit lost its last chain grocery store three years ago [in 2008] when the last two Farmer Jack's groceries closed. This seems incredible—a city of nearly 1 million people without a supermarket—but it's true. No A&P. No Meijer's. Not even a Wal-Mart. Any Detroiters who want fresh store-bought fruits and vegetables or wrapped meats have to get in their car and drive to the suburbs. That is, if they have a car.

In this food desert, some Detroiters have taken to growing their own produce. This has received a great deal of good press from advocates of local food movements, opponents of factory farming, back-to-the-land activists and others who see urban and small-scale farming as the future of American agriculture.

In fact, it's anything but. And we should hope it's anything but.

Urban Farms Show Civic Failure

In Detroit and other cities where these urban farms fill a need, urban farms are nothing less than a symptom of civic catastrophe,

US Food Insecurity Exists

While starvation seldom occurs in [the United States], children and adults do go hungry and chronic mild malnutrition often occurs when financial resources are low. The mental and physical changes that accompany inadequate food intakes can have harmful effects on learning, development, productivity, physical and psychological health, and family life.

Why Hunger, "Domestic Hunger & Federal Food Programs," Food Security Learning Center, *July 2010. www.whyhunger.org.*

a desperate last measure for people trapped in destitute neighborhoods that have become food deserts—places without decent grocery stores, with no local food available except for chips and soda at a convenience shop on the corner.

Most of these people are the descendants of the Southerners who came north to work in the great factories of Detroit and other Northern cities and, not incidentally, to escape sharecropping down South. Most were stranded when those factories collapsed. They have room to farm because fully half the people in the city have moved out.

Yes, these urban plots do grow fresh food. Yes, they provide vegetables to people with no other access to vegetables. Yes, they're definitely better than the alternative, which is nothing.

But to join the foodie chorus in praise of this trend is to misunderstand the whole nature and direction of farming in this country. There are two parallel trends. One is more big farms, of 2,000 acres or more, a trend that has been going on for more than a century. The other is more very small farms, 50 acres or less, serving farmers' markets or specialty shoppers and chefs. (Traditional family farms, the ones in the middle, are vanishing.)

There's nothing wrong with this growth in small farming, so far as it goes: even foodies deserve to eat well. But these niche farms are just that—a niche. With their low yields, they can't possibly meet global demand. And they're off limits to all but urbanites who can afford their higher prices and who have the time to sort through the piles of haricots verts [French green beans] and heirloom tomatoes and then find recipes for them. There's no place in this rarified universe for average people working long hours to afford the lower prices at the local supermarket.

Food Deserts Need Jobs, Not Farms

And as I noted, residents of Detroit don't even have that. Many aren't working at all, which is why they're stuck in those food deserts. Even if they have jobs, it's not possible for them to eat decently by shopping locally.

Those new urban plots are a palliative but no cure. So long as their apologists are allowed to put a positive spin on them, we'll never come close to a solution.

The real solution, of course, is jobs. A vibrant economy produces good housing, good health, and good nutrition for the people who live within it. A broken economy guarantees slums, illness, and malnutrition. As long as Detroit remains an economic wasteland, its food problems cannot be solved.

But short of that, some things can be done. Big box stores—especially Wal-Mart—are beginning to locate in northern cities, if not in the inner city neighborhoods. Because of its savage personnel policies, Wal-Mart faces particular opposition from local politicians. But what if Wal-Mart was allowed to set up a super-store in cities like Detroit—but only if it established smaller groceries, with fresh fruit and vegetables, in the city's food deserts? Empty stores, most of them long off the tax rolls, pock these neighborhoods. The city could give the stores to Wal-

Mart rent-free—but only if it committed to staying for, say, 10 years and to running nutrition classes for local residents.

Wal-Mart is the store that everyone loves to hate, too often for good reason. But if anyone has a better idea, let's hear it. Raising your own rutabagas in vacant lots isn't it.

Periodical and Internet Sources Bibliography

The following articles have been selected to supplement the diverse views presented in this chapter.

Courtney Balestier	"The State of Urban Farming: It Isn't Easy Being Black and Green," *Grio*, July 11, 2011.
Martha Baskin	"Job Training for Homeless and 'at Risk' Youth: Growing Food in the City," *Seattle Post Globe*, May 31, 2011.
Kathy Carr	"Refugee Response Co-founders Say Ohio City Farm Cultivates Northeast Ohio's Economic Vitality, Health," *Crain's Cleveland Business*, February 14, 2011.
Alice Hovorka and Diana Lee Smith	"Gendering the Urban Agriculture Agenda," IDRC, 2006. www.irdc.ca.
Lucy Jarosz	"Nourishing Women: Toward a Feminist Political Ecology of Community Supported Agriculture in the United States," *Gender, Place, and Culture*, June 2011.
Imara Jones	"A Food Crisis Is Coming, but Urban America Already Has It Solved," *Color Lines*, February 16, 2011.
Angelika Kessler, Friedhelm Streiffeler, and Emmanuel Obuobie	"Women in Urban Agriculture in West Africa," *UA Magazine*, May 2004.
Angela Mason and Patsy Benveniste	"Growing Young People from the Ground Up," *Roots*, April 2006.
Amy Tran	"Environmental Youth Alliance: A Conversation with Julia Thiessen," *Soiled and Seeded*, Spring 2011.

OPPOSING
VIEWPOINTS®
SERIES

CHAPTER 4

What Is the Future of Urban Agriculture?

Chapter Preface

Urban farming in the early twenty-first century looks much like rural farming has for centuries: Food is cultivated in plots of land on the earth, in wide-open spaces to maximum exposure to sunlight and rain or in pots and sacks to maximize space. But when engineers and urban planners talk about the future of urban agriculture, what they envision sounds decidedly more similar to science fiction than reality. With the world population expected to reach 7 billion by spring of 2012 and 10 billion by 2050, with 70 percent of that total expected to live in cities, the problem of how to grow adequate food for a rising population will only become more complicated.

According to Rob Goodier, writing in *Popular Mechanics* in June 2010, about 15 percent of food around the world is grown in cities, and that percentage will almost certainly have to rise as urban populations grow over the next several decades and transportation costs increase with the cost of energy. Rooftop gardens are one possible solution to the problem of growing food in cities with little or no vacant land, but in large sizes they are problematic because of the weight they distribute over the top of buildings. One futuristic design by aeronautics engineer and New York University environmental health professor Natalie Jeremijenko features curvy, streamlined greenhouse-like structures mounted on stilts that distribute their weight to a building's load-bearing walls. *Popular Mechanics*' Goodier writes that "to get a streamlined shape, Jeremijenko's design incorporates a skin of ethylene tetrafluoroethylene (ETFE) stretched over curved ribs of steel. ETFE is a supertough, translucent polymer used to cover stadiums and other big spaces. Beneath its skin, the greenhouse is linked to the building below, sharing energy, air and water. Imagine homes and offices where garden-fresh breezes waft through the vents." The design also uses so-called gray water—used water from sinks, bathtubs, and fountains—from the building the greenhouse is mounted to, further improving its environmental sustainability.

Another forward-thinking idea, writes Allison Arieff in *Good* (April 2010), is to reimagine classic American suburbia as a place to grow food, addressing both environmental degradation from overdevelopment and the flagging real estate market. According to Arieff, "In 2008, the New Urbanism evangelist Andrés Duany, of Duany Plater-Zyberk & Company (DPZ), architects and town planners, proclaimed that 'agriculture is the new golf,' a prescient and deliberately provocative claim that is helping frame the conversation about suburbia's future. 'Only 17 percent of people living in golf-course communities play golf more than once a year. Why not grow food?'" The viewpoints in the following chapter debate the future benefits and pitfalls of the new urban agriculture.

| "*Community gardens have become increasingly associated with community building.*"

Urban Agriculture Facilitates Community Building

Shanon C. Kearney

Shanon C. Kearney received her master of landscape architecture degree from the Graduate School of the University of Massachusetts, Department of Landscape Architecture and Regional Planning. In the following viewpoint, Kearney explains that communities ideally need four different kinds of capital to succeed: economic, social, environmental, and human. Kearney argues that all four kinds of capital must be developed simultaneously for optimal success, and that urban agriculture can facilitate this need. Furthermore, Kearney contends, urban planners must consider these needs and develop plans that incorporate space for community gardens, which add long-term value to land, restore natural spaces in urban areas, benefit residents by offering affordable local food, and in general improve the lives of residents and the health of the community by encouraging people to become more engaged and active. Additionally, Kearney concludes, community gardens encourage the building of social networks that allow for the sharing of multicultural and

Shanon C. Kearney, "The Community Garden as a Tool for Community Empowerment: A Study of Community Gardens in Hampden County," Department of Landscape Architecture and Regional Planning, University of Massachusetts, September 2009, pp. 5–10. Copyright © 2009. All rights reserved. Reproduced by permission.

multigenerational values, thereby uniting the larger community and making residents feel more invested over the long term.

As you read, consider the following questions:
1. What were city gardens used for in the 1890s and into the 1960s, according to the author?
2. According to Kearney what percentage of labor is performed by the community in urban gardens, versus city-developed parks?
3. How does the author define "human capital"?

A cross the United States, the creation of sustainable health and wealth in distressed communities is of prime concern to theorists as well as practitioners. Researchers of community greening continue to argue that the community garden's association with nature can have ecologically restorative qualities that translate to economic and social benefits in urban environments. Besides stimulating economic wealth, there are three other forms of capital—social, natural, and human capital—that warrant greater community attention. According to [social scientist Trevor] Hancock, a healthy community is one with high levels of economic, ecological, human, and social 'capital' that in combination can be conceived as 'community capital'. The dilemma confronting communities today is that all four forms need to be addressed simultaneously to have any lasting cumulative benefit. Fortunately, through the development of community gardens, planners and citizens have the power to build long-term community capital even in culturally diverse neighborhoods. As a result, community gardens have become increasingly associated with community building.

Economics Can Hurt Human Capital

In modern capitalist societies, economic wealth is viewed as the primary means by which we obtain our human and social goals.

Communities need to be prosperous in order to feed, clothe, and house their residents, as well as to provide clean water and proper sanitation. Economic capital also provides resources for education, jobs, health, and social services. However, as can be seen in the impact of underregulated land use and development, economic capital can jeopardize the other forms of capital—human, social, or ecological—that also sustain a community's well-being. Fortunately, community gardens can sometimes compensate for economic disinvestment with the production of affordable food where economic capital is limited. After all, a 64-square-foot plot can save a family up to $600 in food purchases per year.

In the 1890s, vacant lot gardens became governmentally sponsored American relief gardens to supplement food supplies in response to the economic downturn. By the 1910s up until the 1960s, vacant lot gardens served war-related needs and efforts to celebrate Americanization in the form of patriotism, conservation, and assimilation of immigrants. Today, the community garden serves a similar economic function: it can alleviate financial pressure for residents of low-income communities by providing cheaper sources of food while promoting self-respect and independence among the poor. However, unlike in 1910, there is a clearer recognition and acceptance of ethnic diversity. By cultivating a community garden, residents can take pride in maintaining a piece of their neighborhood while guaranteeing their survival. Community gardening also allows residents to increase their disposable income by sharing their harvest with a local food bank. In addition, community gardens can also potentially become retail ventures, creating income and employment for the community. For example, in New York City, community gardens have been known sell their herbs to local restaurants. Communities can also earn equity from a community garden, since maintained open space is more valuable than a vacant lot filled with garbage and weeds. In contrast to city-developed parks, gardens are a bargain because they are labor-intensive, and community labor represents 80 percent of the investment

Urban Farming in Detroit

Much has been written about urban farming in Detroit. No one really believes these tiny farms will ever sustain the produce needs of an entire city, but few doubt that they will continue to play an important role in the city's transformation and they will only grow in importance as an integral part of the city's food culture. The vegetables and fruits grown in Detroit's gardens are so bountiful that neighborhood produce stands pop up; a coalition of inner-city gardeners sells thousands of pounds of affordable produce almost daily during the growing season at local farmer's markets. Soup kitchens and schools supply their own produce from extensive and expertly farmed plots. In 2010, several Detroit farmers banded together to start the first CSA [Community Supported (or Shared) Agriculture] deliveries consisting entirely of produce grown in the city. Small-scale farming in Detroit has actually become a viable part of the urban food system and not just a novelty as it is in other cities.

James Griffioen, "Detroit Resident Calls
Bullshit on 'Food Desert' Propaganda,"
ReclaimDemocracy.org, January 24, 2011.

in the project. Overall, community gardens are a wise financial investment especially when compared to the alternatives of vacancy and neglect.

Encouraging Ecological Capital

From the ecological capital perspective, community gardens are vibrant alternatives to vacant lots or commercial developments. As research shows, gardens provide a restorative green retreat for the urban dweller who is typically plagued by stress and fatigue. With their flowers and other plants, community gardens also serve as habitats for various birds and insects. Gardens help cool the city by utilizing solar energy, both in photosynthesis and in evaporating water from the foliage and soil. Likewise, if gardeners establish a vegetable garden, the food grown will likely be organic which suggests the possibility of composting. As a result, a community garden can help to reduce the amount of waste a community produces. Finally, since the food is grown locally, there is no need to ship long distances. The community garden effectively contributes to the ecological capital of the community. Therefore, community residents can experience ecology as dynamically linked to their urban environment. Urban agriculture can return nature to cities to help restore the connection to natural processes that has been obscured by mechanization.

Gardening as a Teaching Tool

Human capital relates to healthy, well-educated, skilled, creative people who become involved with their community and local governance. When community gardens are established, there is potential for people to learn directly about gardening and about other cultures, as well as about the environment, organic farming, different cooking techniques, and the nutritional value of food. A community garden offers the potential of intergenerational learning whereby more experienced gardeners can teach less experienced ones. Gardens can be used by adults to mentor children and to introduce them to the natural processes of growth, maturation, and decay and to social processes of cooperation and collective effort. Tending a garden can also convey a feeling of pride and joy, a sense of personal growth, and the opportunity for self-sufficiency to residents of public housing. Human interaction in the garden can build human capital by fostering community through shared projects and by improving the nutritional status of the community with the introduction of fresh food. Different types of activity within the community garden—such as visits with friends, neighborhood gatherings, nature education, recycling, and composting, board games, art classes, performances, yoga and childcare—all show that community gardens can spur neighborhood revitalization.

Building a Social Network

To understand the social function of the community garden in the urban landscape, a researcher must recognize the importance of community contributions. Communities create and manage gardens largely by themselves. From the start, the community garden depends upon a unified social network to organize and manage its program and access. People often congregate to work, relax, and enjoy communal spaces, and through these interactions build community. In ethnically diverse neighborhoods, there is a tendency for families to grow the foods that are culturally familiar. As a social space, gardens serve as a medium for the transport and translation of cultural practices that concern both nature and food. Different ethnic groups can use the community garden to cultivate and prepare foods as they would in their homeland. Eventually, other families may develop an interest in the vegetables other cultures grow and use. Consequently, there is the potential for ethnic groups to begin sharing planting practices, foods, recipes, or establishing community potlucks that build social networks across ethno-racial lines.

Gardening and socializing make people feel that they are part of the community and part of the land. Unfortunately, cultural exchange and interaction are not always an assured outcome. What has yet to be determined is whether community gardens can be planned and managed to further encourage an organic growth of social capital. Community gardens serve as an interpretative mediation between nature and culture with regard to the nutritional needs, medicinal purposes, religious beliefs, aesthetic preferences, and land resource uses of different ethnic groups. When overlaid with the notion of fostering community, community gardens become even more complicated entities. Additional research is required to determine what types of planning and management practices encourage social interaction and build community without causing cultural isolation.

Gardening Is a Political Act

Finally, community gardens can act as springboards to other forms of social and economic activity. For example, city gardens can help communities reclaim their neighborhoods from crime and pollution, and save kids from risks on the street. By encouraging the involvement of the homeless, community gardens can help them with access to food, job connections, and social ties with local residents. Likewise, interest in community gardens can foster interest in larger food systems agriculture that promote community capital on different scales, such as bulk-buying groups, food co-ops, or community supported agriculture.

In order to understand the possibility of building community capital, however, it is crucial to begin by examining the role of grassroots urban politics in the making of the public realm. Marti Ross Bjornson, a graduate student at Northwestern University, found that the process of community gardening is ultimately a political activity. Bjornson concluded that by simply starting a garden, previously powerless people can learn how to gain access to city power including public policy, economic resources, and social interaction. As a result, many community gardens serve to grow responsible garden leaders while simultaneously encouraging wider civic participation. Today, the success of most community gardens requires the combined efforts of local garden leaders, members of not-for-profit technical support organizations, and, in the case of city-leased gardens, city officials. With the understanding that urban gardens provide areas with a "sense of community" that may lead to "increased involvement in neighborhood issues," suitable methods for measuring community capital become apparent. For instance, reduced littering rates and improved maintenance of other properties in a neighborhood associated with a community garden suggest that increased community capital can be documented.

"As agriculture returns to cities, it is important to identify and manage the problems that it could potentially cause."

Urban Agriculture Poses Health and Safety Issues

John E. Mogk, Sarah Kwiatkowski, and Mary J. Weindorf

In the following viewpoint, the authors examine the wider implications of urban agriculture for present and future generations of people living in communities with fairly large-scale farming projects. According to the authors, possible future problems include water contamination and scarcity, air pollution, and generation of harmful waste materials. A major initial problem for potential farms, the authors note, is existing soil contamination, especially from lead, which is commonly found in urban soils. Livestock presents another issue, the authors point out, with the potential for waste problems as well as noise and nuisance issues, particularly with chickens and other fowl; methane produced by cattle is another possible source of contamination in the form of poor air quality. And any use of pesticides on nonorganic farms, the authors contend, can present serious health problems for both current and future residents. Finally, the authors conclude, physical safety may be an issue, with the movement of large farm equipment through crowded city streets presenting a possible road hazard, and noise from equipment proving bothersome to residents. John E. Mogk is a professor of law at Wayne State University in Detroit, Michigan. He has provided counsel to government officials on matters related to housing and community development. Sarah Kwiatkowski is an attorney in private practice in Seattle, Washington, who provides pro bono services for the Housing Justice Project. Mary J. Weindorf is production editor of the Wayne State Law Review.

As you read, consider the following questions:

1. What are some kinds of soil contaminants other than lead that are mentioned by the authors?
2. According to the authors, how does lead contamination spread to humans working in farming?
3. What are the main animal contaminants that cause concern in cattle farming, as stated by the authors?

Cities promote the public health, safety, morals, and general welfare through zoning. Zoning allows cities to effectively coordinate land uses among neighboring landowners and resolve community conflicts before they occur. It is the principal tool to address any problems associated with urban agriculture. However, local zoning in Michigan of "commercial production of farm products" is preempted by the provisions of the state's Right to Farm Act. . . .

As cities expanded and absorbed surrounding open space and farmland, agricultural uses were phased out and eventually excluded altogether from the master plans and zoning ordinances of most cities. Today, however, expanding areas of vacant land in declining cities, such as Detroit, have little demand for traditional urban uses, and offer a renewed opportunity to promote agriculture. However, as agriculture returns, it is important to identify and manage the problems that agriculture—especially as it is conventionally practiced in more rural areas—could potentially cause in cities.

Environmental Concerns

Environmental concerns with respect to urban agriculture relate to soil contamination, contamination of ground and surface waters, air pollution, increased water demand, potentially higher load on sewage systems, and the potential for the production of harmful waste materials. Some agricultural wastes, if properly managed, can be beneficially recycled through composting or transformation into fuel. The management process can be costly, however.

Risks related to soil contamination include: the potential that plants will absorb or transport contaminants, that groundwater will become contaminated, and that bioaccumulation will occur when livestock or humans ingest contaminated crops. While certain chemicals naturally exist in soils, many are toxic at high concentrations. The ideal situation for production of agriculture products occurs where the contamination in soil does not exceed natural levels. Lead is particularly hazardous and is found naturally in soils at a level of 10 parts per million (p.p.m.). The EPA [US Environmental Protection Agency] standard for unsafe levels caused by lead contamination is 400 p.p.m. There is the likelihood that a number of plots in Detroit do not meet the EPA standard. Other contaminants with which to be concerned include: zinc, PAHs [paracyclic aromatic hydrocarbons], chromium, copper, molybdenum, sulfur, cadmium, copper, zinc, PBTs [polybutylated terephthalates], benzene, toluene, xylene, arsenic, mercury (historical use), chlordane and other chlorinated pesticides.

The principal risk in urban gardens is from lead-contaminated soil or dust clinging to the plants as they are handled or ingested, which is especially significant for young people working in gardens, for whom the EPA appropriately places a lower threshold given their development stage. It is also a major concern for urban agriculture because plants absorb lead through their leaves and from the soil. Lead contamination is documented as widespread in Detroit. It is important to learn more about and support existing community-based efforts to help gardeners test for lead and undertake measures to minimize exposure through direct contact with soil containing lead or indirectly through ingestion of plant materials that may have taken up lead. Building raised beds with clean soil is one such method, and knowledgeable gardeners such as those in existing gardening programs already use this and other related methods. Atmospheric pollution of gardens by lead is an understudied issue and also needs attention.

Existing Lead Contamination

Detroit soil contains lead from lead paint chips and lead dust from remnants of older demolished buildings, emissions from lead based gasoline engines, and air borne lead contaminants from the city's industry. Detroit is not alone in facing lead contamination. Recently, hazardous amounts of lead have been documented in the backyards and communities of such other major cities as New York, Baltimore, Boston, Chicago, Los Angeles, Minneapolis, and Philadelphia. A study shows that between 1950 and 1984 cars and trucks in Michigan emitted about 182,000 metric tons of lead and that in the year 2000 alone, Michigan companies legally released 24,345 pounds of lead and lead compounds. The concern is great because lead does not evaporate, so harmful contaminates emitted long ago remain in Detroit's soil. The problem is particularly acute as it relates to children who have a five times greater lead absorption rate than adults. Lead builds up in the body over years, and many of Detroit's children already have elevated levels from lead exposure since birth.

A recent study done by the Detroit Department of Health & Wellness and the Detroit Public Schools [DPS] had startling results—of the 39,000 DPS children tested, fifty-eight percent had a history of lead poisoning. The study also showed that a link exists between high levels of lead present in children and low-test scores within Detroit Public Schools. The study further found a link between high levels of lead and children within the Detroit Public Schools system that needed special education. Prime contributors to contamination in the Detroit area include former gas stations and industrial sites. Contamination is also more likely to result if property use currently or in the past involved the application of lead paint, use or production of fertilizer or pesticides, commercial activity, treated lumber, machine repair, junk vehicles, furniture refinishing, fires, landfills, garbage dumps, or the property is in a high traffic area.

If hazardous levels of lead are detected, these risks can be managed by soil remediation after testing. The two principal approaches are mixing or covering the high lead soil with clean soil or physically removing and replacing the lead soil. In addition, select crops, such as sunflowers, have the ability to absorb and remove lead from the soil.

Livestock Contamination

Pesticides, fertilizers, and untreated manure can, also contaminate farming soils. Corn, wheat, and soybeans, which are usually used for feed crops, are the first, second, and fourth leading consumers of fertilizer. Disposal and treatment of manure, unlike human waste, is not regulated by any standards and, as a result, untreated manure can be carried away by rainwater into feedlots, pastures, and water sources for human or animal consumption. . . .

Raising cattle in urban areas can cause serious air and water quality issues. Cattle produce gaseous pollutants, which add to the already poor air quality present in urban areas. Four animal contaminants in particular have been identified as problems related to raising cattle in urban areas: methane, reactive organic compounds, ammonia, and hazardous matter.

The use of pesticides is also a concern due to the drift that occurs both during and after application. The U.S. Environmental Protection Agency regulates pesticide spray and dust drift recognizing that "pesticide applications can expose people, wildlife, and the environment to pesticide residue that can cause health and environmental effects and property damage." While the EPA and the Michigan Department of Agriculture have set forth guidelines for the application of pesticides to reduce the amount of drift that occurs from their application, neither regulation prohibits drift entirely.

Water Contamination and Scarcity

The Environmental Protection Agency estimates that "agriculture generates pollutants that degrade aquatic life" and interfere with thousands of miles of river. Agriculture and productions "contributes to seventy percent of all water quality problems identified in rivers and streams." Farms generate both liquid and solid waste that pose high risks for water sources, and in the urban setting there is a greater risk of chemical contamination in dense areas. Furthermore, attention must be paid to the unregulated use of un-composted solids and untreated water that is often used to irrigate crops or to feed animals.

Producing meat consumes a large amount of water, and animals need water to drink for hydration and cooling. An average of one thousand gallons of irrigation water is needed to produce approximately one pound of protein. Agriculture in an urban setting introduces a competitor for clean water. While access to clean water in Detroit on its face is not a problem because the system has a hugely underutilized capacity, use of the system's water for urban agriculture should not deplete nor otherwise negatively affect water supplies for Detroit residents. . . .

Noise and Safety Issues

Agriculture equipment can cause problems when driven on urban roads and can increase noise pollution. Generally, the term "agriculture equipment" is meant to include: tractors, self-propelled machines, and equipment that may be towed by or attached to tractors or self-propelled machines and excludes vehicles not used in the production of agriculture.

Even in rural areas, usual motor vehicle traffic encounters problems when sharing the roads with agriculture equipment. One of the main concerns is driver safety. In crashes involving farm vehicles, the farm vehicle occupant is killed almost twice as often as occupants of the other vehicle. Most collisions occur during planting and harvesting seasons, with a majority of crashes occuring between 3:00 and 6:00 P.M. A Texas report states that common crashes between agriculture equipment and usual motor vehicle traffic include: rear end, left turn, passing, crossroads, and oncoming collisions.

The two most common causes of collisions are that public roads are not wide enough for agriculture equipment and few traffic laws properly address issues related to agriculture equipment on public roads. For example, many traffic laws do not address proper lighting and marking of agriculture equipment for other drivers on the road.

Introducing agriculture equipment contributes to urban noise pollution. Noise from agriculture equipment, like the loud persistent drone of a tractor engine, will be unfamiliar and unpopular to city dwellers. There is a need to address potential conflicts with agriculture noises through proper time, manner, and place regulations. Larger trucks that may be needed to move agricultural inputs as well as to harvest products and wastes may also cause problems. In addition, problems may be created due to the traffic capacity within urban neighborhoods, air pollution, noise pollution, smells, and conflicts with pedestrian and other traffic.

Livestock in the City

Raising livestock in the city is highly contentious because cities are places of dense populations. An important first step should be to define at the outset what a municipality means by the term "livestock" to properly distinguish it from "domestic animals." Boise, Idaho, has a helpful definition: "Livestock . . . are defined as having a commercial use. [T]hese animals are typically raised to sell their products such as wool, milk, meat and pelts." Another good model is that of the Midwest Environmental Advocates, which defines "livestock" by listing specific animals. Those include: cows, cattle, sheep, goats, hogs, horses, mules, and poultry. Not clearly defining the animals will cause difficulties in enforcing regulations.

Noises, smells, or other animal-related annoyances that affect neighbors and other adjacencies must be addressed. Additionally, animals may transmit diseases affecting the public health. Animal excrement not properly managed decomposes producing an odor, and increasing the number of bacteria and flies. For example, "Animal dung is a source of tetanus . . . especially if the animals are left outside to graze—a phenomenon often seen in the city." The runoff from animal waste products, associated with dairy cattle, chicken sheds, and pig pens, pollutes surrounding areas and attracts "disease causing vectors, such as mosquitoes." Additionally, raising livestock in urban areas can overwhelm sewage systems and contaminate water supplies. Detroit's sewage system, however, reportedly has excess treatment capacity.

An important criterion for examining the problems associated with urban livestock is the scale and degree of commercialization. Distinctions between different systems have been categorized as (1) subsistence backyard (or personal use); (2) semi-commercial (including community gardens); and (3) large-scale commercial systems. Large-scale commercial systems having livestock are potentially the most problematic because they produce large amounts of waste such as excrement and urine.

Chickens and other fowl raise issues of nuisance, including noise, un-cleanliness from excrement and smell, unsightly coop construction, rodents, and disease. Furthermore, the health and well being of the chicken must be considered. Other fowl, such as roosters, are extremely noisy and are generally prohibited by zoning regulations. However, many engaged in agriculture acknowledge other benefits of keeping roosters, such as their fertilization of eggs, which increases lecithin, an agent that counteracts cholesterol. Many health advocates seek fertilized eggs, thereby creating a market for them. A zoning ordinance should allow roosters in residential areas as long as the zoning ordinance restricts the number of roosters to an appropriate hen/rooster ratio, and also protects the neighboring residents from excessive noise.

Rearing and pasturing large animals in the city raises several potential problems: (1) many acres are needed to humanely pasture the animals; (2) there are significant impacts on human health and the environment; and (3) problems relating to nuisance such as noise, smell, and aesthetics. Raising bovines [cattle] requires particularly large tracts of land. It is possible to raise one dairy cow for personal consumption. However, if a plan is to include large-scale commercial dairy farming or beef cattle raising, planners need to consider a space-to-animal ratio, which provides for overall health and safety of the animal, and ensures that products from city-raised animals do not to pose a threat to human health.

"*For models of planning and community development, we look to the leading urban farming and community gardening programs.*"

Urban Planners Should Look to Community Farms for City Design Models

Domenic Vitiello and Michael Nairn

Domenic Vitiello is an assistant professor of city and regional planning at the University of Pennsylvania. Michael Nairn is a lecturer in urban studies at the University of Pennsylvania. In the following viewpoint, the authors address the vast difference between trends in urban planning for "vertical" farms and exotic crops in major international cities—intended for maximum corporate profit—with the reality of urban agriculture as it currently exists in cities in the United States and Europe. The authors discuss the history and present state of urban gardening in Philadelphia, noting that despite a lack of institutional support, neighborhoods with community-run gardens have shown stronger cohesion and resiliency than those without gardens. Vitiello and Nairn assert that all residents engaged in community gardening are essentially entrepreneurs adding to their local economies, whether they garden for profit or not,

Domenic Vitiello and Michael Nairn, "Everyday Urban Agriculture: From Community Gardening to Community Food Security," *Harvard Design Magazine*, Fall/Winter, 2009–2010. Copyright © 2010. All rights reserved. Reproduced by permission.

simply due to the value gardens add to the community. What is lacking in the plans of large-scale vertical farming, contend Vitiello and Nairn, is the quality of life provided by the urban gardening experience. Urban planners, the authors maintain, should model their developments on the type of farming being done in cities like Philadelphia, Detroit, and Milwaukee in order to maximize that quality of life for communities.

As you read, consider the following questions:

1. What do the authors cite as the valuable agricultural re-sources available in inner cities?
2. What is vertical farming, according to Vitiello and Nairn?
3. Why do the authors say vertical farms are impractical for cities like Philadelphia, Detroit, and Chicago?

Large scale and professional planning and design for urban agriculture and sustainable food systems are in a speculative phase, at least in the global North. Designers understandably fancy vivid renderings projecting skyscraper farms or golden fields of wheat and acres of corn across vast swaths of the in-ner city. Our architecture and planning students dream of in-serting Havana's roof gardens, community farms, and corner produce stands into Pittsburgh and New Orleans. The impulse seems right, since scaling up urban agriculture holds real poten-tial for restoring local ecology, economies, and health, and we have much to learn from the experience of cities in the global South (see in particular the work of the Resource Centers for Urban Agriculture and Food Security in Africa, South America, and Asia). But there are good reasons why our designs for multi-million dollar "vertical" farms and bulk commodity—or worse, tropical—crops in Manhattan and Chicago have not been built or tested. They have little grounding in the reality—and pleasure—of sustainable urban agriculture, which is solidly grounded in local climates and soils.

The reality is that most urban agriculture in the United States, Canada, and Europe takes the form of community gardening. This is an "everyday urbanism," largely disconnected from the world of professional design. Far from our dreams of vertical farming or vast tracts of cropland, today's city farms plant higher-value vegetables intensively in limited space, growing vastly more food per acre than do industrial farms. Yet urban agriculture in the global North remains an economically marginal activity, typically subsisting with the aid of philanthropists.

A Rich History

The inner city presents our greatest challenges for food security, but it is not without agricultural assets. Growing food connects people to their environment and to their neighbors, nurturing trust and relationships that tie together social, economic, and ecological systems. Many people garden as a deliberate strategy to feed people who lack regular access to fresh, nutritious food. Community gardens in Philadelphia concentrate overwhelmingly in low-wealth neighborhoods ravished by disinvestment, where people do their best in circumstances that most Americans would find intolerable. Often poor people are repositories of vast agricultural knowledge, since a large (although shrinking) proportion of gardeners arrived via the Great Migrations of African Americans and Puerto Ricans or later waves of immigrants from farming regions of the world. This knowledge is a rich, largely unreported ore in poor communities; it counters the images of the "inner city" offered by the evening news or TV shows like *The Wire*. Many of the social networks in these neighborhoods are surprisingly resilient, often coalescing around food production sites.

A dozen years ago, Philadelphia was home to the most robust urban gardening support system in the United States: The Pennsylvania Horticultural Society and Penn State Agricultural Extension supported 500 food-producing gardens and hundreds more that grew flowers and shade trees. In the 1980s and '90s, the rationale for these programs lay in helping bring people to-gether to take back vacant lots and build community in places devastated by deindustrialization. During the economic boom of the late '90s, public and philanthropic dollars for these programs were withdrawn, and their support system mostly dismantled. Today, the Horticultural Society supports roughly forty commu-nity gardens and three farms through the City Harvest Program, which delivers seedlings raised in the Philadelphia County Prison greenhouse to gardeners who set aside plots to grow vegetables they deliver to local food banks. This is the formal side of com-munity gardens' role in building local food security. Yet there is a much larger *informal* side of food security in gardens not sup-ported by any institution, since gardeners have proven remark-ably resilient in the face of declining support. This is the story of most community gardening in Philadelphia. . . .

Experimenting with Crops and Land

Most urban farms are experimental, searching for the right com-bination of funding, products, and programs that will ensure their success. The oldest in Philadelphia, Greensgrow Farm, is celebrating its tenth anniversary. Located on the site of a former steel galvanizing plant, it grows lettuce and basil hydroponically, heirloom tomatoes in raised beds, and potted plants in green-houses. Greensgrow has diversified its activities to include a Community Supported Agriculture (CSA) arrangement with a network of rural farms, farm stand, vermicomposting, biodiesel production, a new community kitchen, and its Honey from the Hood. It supplies mostly middle-class pleasures, as does Weavers Way Farm, located in a historic arboretum, although Weavers Way also supports Martin Luther King [MLK] High School Farm, whose students sell their produce at the City Hall Farmers' Market. One of the student farmers at MLK found happiness in discovering that sorrel tastes like sour apple Skittles.

The future of urban agriculture is at these farms and oth-ers like them on vacant lots, parkland, and in the densest cities

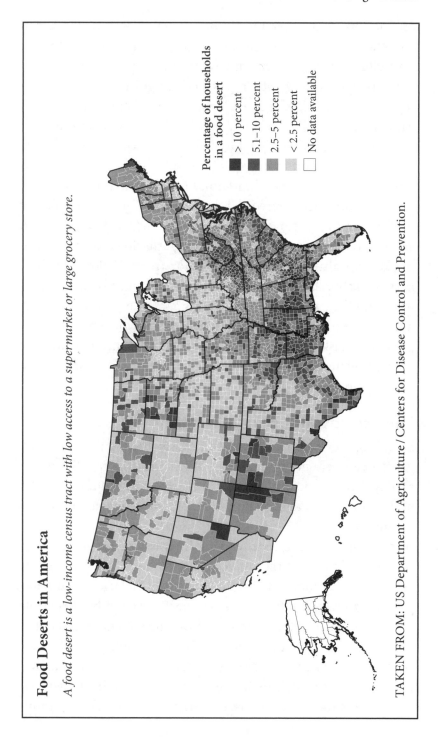

Food Deserts in America

A food desert is a low-income census tract with low access to a supermarket or large grocery store.

Percentage of households
in a food desert

▮ > 10 percent

▮ 5.1–10 percent

▮ 2.5–5 percent

▯ < 2.5 percent

▯ No data available

TAKEN FROM: US Department of Agriculture / Centers for Disease Control and Prevention.

on rooftops and other mostly horizontal spaces of the urban landscape. But it is also in the community gardens that make up a vital if sometimes not as sexy part of city food production. Some people go to great lengths to distinguish between "farming" and "gardening," but we believe this distinction has little value if creating food security and local economies is our goal. Many of the gardeners we met call themselves "farmers," only some jokingly. Community gardens make significant contributions to household and community food economies, and some gardeners we encountered sell their harvest. Indeed, one family in Philadelphia's second largest allotment garden grows as much as the city's third biggest farm, selling at a downtown farmers' market but also giving much away for free to fellow parishioners at its church, We also submit that the hundreds of gardeners who tend their plots with the express goal of providing food for hungry friends, family, and strangers are performing an entrepreneurial task. While they may not profit financially, most are duly compensated by the profound pleasure of sharing health and happiness through food.

The Real Joys of Urban Agriculture

Spending some down and dirty time in the local community garden can help get designers in touch with the realities of everyday urban agriculture. It will likely make the enterprise seem both more challenging and more pleasurable than they had imagined.

Recently we have watched with interest and amusement the extensive media coverage of vertical farming. Finally, designers are integrating food into urban projects. In alluring computer-generated images, futuristic skyscrapers powered by renewable energy sources recycle wastewater from the entire city and house production systems that can feed 50,000 people in completely controlled antiseptic conditions. What's not to like? As our dystopic colleague Catherine Bonier pointed out, "What they never show you is the basement where furnaces and bunks for immigrant workers sit cheek by jowl." One can imagine the *ConAgra Tower* or *Archer Daniels Midland Food Production Center* dominating the skyline of Manhattan—such companies may be the only ones with the capital to build these towers. In the paranoid fantasy of science fiction writers, one can see the *Soylent Green Tower* producing a continuous diet of Happy Meals for the satiated residents of New York.

Vertical farming is handicapped: It is a capital-intensive strategy for a labor-intensive industry. It may make sense for Dubai, the new eco-city of Dongtan, or perhaps Midtown Manhattan someday, but not for Philadelphia, Detroit, or Chicago, where both land and labor are abundant.

What is more difficult to imagine in skyscraper farms is the quality of life we found at many community gardens and urban farms. The Philadelphia experience is a more ordinary story than agriculture in hermetically sealed towers designed by starchitects or tropical roof gardens across Havana. But it is a more real story for United States cities in particular. It is the story of everyday, organic urbanism in which people alter their own neighborhoods in both surprising and mundane ways. It is also the story of people's efforts to overcome deindustrialization and its devastating consequent ills: unemployment, poverty, hunger, obesity, asthma, and crime.

Our own speculative proposal for feeding the global North builds on the Philadelphia experience. For models of planning and community development, we look to the leading urban farming and community gardening programs of Vancouver, Detroit, Milwaukee, and Kansas City; and to Britain, to Middlesbrough's Town Meal designed by André Viljoen and Katrin Bohn, and to London's new Capital Growth campaign. This last effort is not a financial scheme but rather an effort to harness the energies of citizens and community organizations to grow food in 2,012 new urban spaces by the year 2012. We envision more processing and canning to preserve the summer's bounty and low-tech greenhouses to keep food growing through the winter. We imagine the emergence of a more humane city in which relationships and the exchange of food and agricultural traditions are valued, whether cash changes hands or not. Urban agriculture is a solution based more on people than on technology. It is more "kitchen capitalism" than financial capitalism. It will not be a panacea or a quick fix. It will be, however, one important stock in the portfolio of how people in cities feed themselves and each other in the future, and derive pleasure from the experience.

> *"The benefits of turning lawns into fresh fruits and vegetables . . . are colliding with city rules designed to protect . . . cherished neighborhoods."*

Urban Farmers Collide with City Rules

Lynn Horsley

Lynn Horsley is a reporter for the Kansas City Star, *a Missouri daily newspaper. In the following viewpoint, Horsley addresses the problems sometimes caused by farming in urban areas, especially with for-profit ventures in areas zoned neither for farming nor business. In Kansas City, Missouri, writes Horsley, city farms have become ubiquitous and profitable, although in some cases the regulatory issues and annoyance of neighbors have led to serious legal problems involving the city council. Of chief concern, Horsley notes, is creating a balance between the desire of city government to designate Kansas City a "green" city and the aspects of urban farming that many consider a nuisance. Local preservationists argue that residential neighborhoods must maintain their primary purpose of providing living spaces, not growing crops or running businesses. Livestock has become a particularly contentious issue, with neighbors of urban gardeners taking issue with the presence of chickens, goats, and other farming animals in residential neighborhoods, Horsley notes, and traffic presents another problem when urban farmers begin to sell their products out of their homes.*

As you read, consider the following questions:
1. Why are apprentices not allowed to work at BadSeed Farm, according to the author?
2. Why do some residents object to having farms in residential neighborhoods, as reported by Horsley?
3. Why are many city leaders in favor of developing urban farms, according to the author?

Kansas City, MO (AP)—Steve Mann doesn't look like an outlaw as he cheerfully harvests giant rutabagas and luscious lettuce bunches from a friend's garden in Kansas City, North.

But technically he is violating Kansas City ordinances as he prepares to sell the produce.

Brooke Salvaggio never dreamed that she and her husband, Dan Heryer, were running afoul of city codes when they used a few apprentices in their backyard garden business in south Kansas City.

These foot soldiers in the urban farming revolution have found that, along with locally grown food, they are cultivating a controversy.

While they try to capitalize on blossoming awareness about the benefits of turning lawns into fresh fruits and vegetables, they are colliding with city rules designed to protect Kansas City's cherished neighborhoods.

Those are rules that the city will be rethinking. But for now, Mann is not allowed to sell produce from a residential property he does not own.

And Salvaggio and Heryer are not allowed to use apprentices in their garden business, dubbed BadSeed Farm, because city codes prohibit outside employees at home occupations.

Issues of Concern for City Leaders

Among the thorny questions for planners, policy makers, practitioners, and members of the public include: the appropriate scale of urban agriculture; whether food production should be interspersed throughout the city, form a contiguous productive landscape, or be concentrated on the periphery; whether food processing and sales are appropriate in residential neighborhoods; and more broadly whether food production deserves to be treated differently than other types of businesses.

Nevin Cohen, "Chicago's Urban Agriculture Zoning Proposal," Urban Food Policy, *January 6, 2011.*

Urban farming is an issue confronting cities all over the country.

How can they regulate gardening as a home-based business? And how can they manage the chickens, goats and other livestock that enhance a farming operation but prompt complaints about noise and odor from nearby residents?

In this area, people are hoping the Kansas City Council will take the lead in balancing these competing interests. "Because of Kansas City's desire to be a green city," City Planner Patty Noll said, "this council has directed us to make (urban agriculture) a priority."

Not so fast, says Dona Boley, a neighborhood and historic preservation advocate. She grew up on a farm outside Paola, Kan., and says agriculture doesn't easily mix with many residential parts of town.

"We want to protect residential neighborhoods," she said.

In June, the Overland Park City Council denied a permit for four backyard hens despite testimonials about fresh eggs.

St. Louis is looking at outlawing roosters. Wyandotte County is considering some livestock restrictions after complaints about horses.

Yet across the country, many communities are welcoming urban agriculture for its small-business potential, especially in economically deprived areas riddled with underused vacant properties.

"Cities are looking at it as much as an economic development issue as a hobby or recreation," said Alfonso Morales, a University of Wisconsin assistant professor of urban and regional planning who has studied local agricultural initiatives.

Among examples Morales cited: Cleveland and Boston allow urban agriculture districts within their city limits. Sacramento, Calif., has relaxed its rules about front-yard vegetable plantings.

Kansas City is not necessarily unfriendly to urban farmers. It has relatively liberal rules governing chickens and some other aspects of producing local food, noted Katherine Kelly, executive director of the Kansas City Center for Urban Agriculture, which has helped about 50 area urban farms.

But as the movement gains momentum, Kelly said she thought Kansas City's code could be even more progressive and serve as a model for other cities.

Judging from the 100 people who packed a late October meeting at Salvaggio's and Heryer's BadSeed Farmer's Market, 1909 McGee St., the urban farming movement here has a lot of support. City Councilman John Sharp, whose district includes Salvaggio's backyard farm near Bannister and State Line roads, told the crowd that he thought Kansas City could tweak its rules on gardening businesses. He said the city would also look at modifying its restrictions on chickens and livestock, although he admitted that was likely to be more contentious.

"We don't want to generate constant traffic, but if we allow people to grow vegetables for more than their own use, there has to be some way for them to sell them," Sharp said in an interview.

"I think urban farming is an inevitable trend in the U.S. I think we can encourage more urban agriculture without destabilizing neighborhoods. In fact, if it's done right, this will enhance neighborhoods."

In Kansas City, gardeners can have up to 15 chickens and even two goats—if they meet certain distance restrictions from structures.

But as Salvaggio and Heryer found out when someone this summer called animal control, three goats can get you in trouble. (The urban farmers say three goats are more content than two.)

An August public hearing about the goats prompted the city to review its rules—and provoked passionate views from opponents and supporters.

"My wife and I strongly object to the use of this property for multiple goats," witness Barry Seward testified. "And certainly, we have concerns about chickens and other wildlife or animals in the neighborhood."

Supporters argued the 1-acre garden was a community asset and that the three goats were cleaner and better behaved than most dogs.

"It is a beautiful piece of property," witness Jane Carol said, adding that it was a better use of the land than just a lawn.

Salvaggio and Heryer lost their appeal and sent the goats to a rural farm in Kansas. They subsequently learned about the rules prohibiting apprentices and barring customers from picking up their produce on-site. They are complying with those rules but are not sure they can run a successful farm under such constraints next spring.

Urban farmer Steve Mann, active in a Kansas City group Food Not Lawns, said the BadSeed Farm was the "poster child" for why Kansas City's rules needed to be changed.

"This is how you build community," he said.

Yet Boley, the neighborhood advocate, wondered where Kansas City would draw the line if it relaxed its rules for small commercial produce operations in residential areas.

"If you're selling, it's like you have a nursery, or a kennel," she said. "It's like parking a business down in a residential neighborhood. Business rules need to apply."

Boley knows from her childhood on a farm that the issues concerning chickens, rabbits and other livestock are even more difficult.

"Chicken (excrement) is everywhere," she said. "I don't think it's appropriate within residential zones."

Carol Winterowd, a past neighborhood president who lives two blocks from the BadSeed Farm, also wants to ensure that Kansas City doesn't jeopardize neighborhood stability.

"Everyone has their own picture of what a neighborhood should look like," she said. "I just want to be sure the neighborhood quality of life is not compromised."

Morales, the assistant professor, said urban agriculture needn't threaten strong residential character and could increase property values. There are ways to impose distance and setback requirements, landscape screening guidelines and other restrictions to limit animal impact and make sure gardens don't become unsightly, he said.

Sharp said he believed the city could deal with the home-based business issues before the next planting season, although animal issues may take longer.

Salvaggio and Heryer said they may need to find a new location with more acreage to run their business successfully. But they have no intention of disappearing into the country. Heryer said the urban farming debate could educate the public and benefit the community.

"It doesn't have to be a point of division," he said. "It can be a point of unity."

| "Urban agriculture should be evaluated based on . . . the many services or benefits that can be provided by agricultural land uses."

Urban Agriculture Provides Communities with More Benefits than Just Food

Sarah Taylor Lovell

Sarah Taylor Lovell is an assistant professor of sustainable landscape design in the Department of Crop Sciences, University of Illinois. In the following viewpoint, Lovell maintains that agricultural pursuits are inherently multifunctional, serving several purposes other than producing consumable products, but urban developers and planners should emphasize these functions to get the most use out of agricultural projects in cities. According to Lovell, while the appeal of local food is a built-in benefit to urban agriculture, planners also must take into account the ecological and cultural functions that farming in city centers can offer. Additionally, city and regional planners have the capacity to incorporate appropriate zoning to accommodate agricultural projects into developments and to avoid future problems and disputes. Lovell states that taking into account "food systems" when designing urban spaces allows planners

Sarah Taylor Lovell, "Multifunctional Urban Agriculture for Sustainable Land Use Planning in the United States," *Sustainability*, August 2010, pp. 2500–2503. Copyright © 2010. All rights reserved. Reproduced by permission.

to take into account other potential future problems related to disaster planning, giving urban residents easy access to food even in the event of a natural or human-made disaster. Other issues that should fall within the purview of urban planners, Lovell concludes, include transportation systems to ensure that residents have a way to get to their food sources and food networks to connect growers with potential buyers.

As you read, consider the following questions:

1. What are the "ecological functions" and "cultural functions" offered by urban agriculture, according to the author?
2. What are the "urban agriculture activities" cited by Lovell?
3. Why does urban agriculture offer more opportunities for social and cultural interaction than rural agriculture, according to Lovell?

Because of the high value of land and many competing land use needs in cities, agriculture may not initially seem like a wise alternative for urban settings. In fact, certain production systems would be completely inappropriate for this environment, such as those requiring large tracts of land, relying heavily on inputs of petrochemicals, or creating negative externalities for the surrounding environment (e.g., conventional grain production or livestock confinement systems). For an urban environment, agricultural production systems that take advantage of the close proximity of resources and consumers, such as those offering fresh, value-added, specialty products would be most appropriate. Systems providing food that can be directly consumed by nearby residents could offer many benefits for growers, consumers, and the community. However, even with these systems, justifying the use of urban land for agriculture based on the production functions alone can be a challenge. Instead, urban agriculture should be evaluated based on a framework of landscape multifunctionality, which accounts for the many services or benefits that can be provided by agricultural land uses. In addition to production functions, urban agriculture offers a wide range of ecological functions (e.g., biodiversity, nutrient cycling, and micro-climate control) and cultural functions (e.g., recreation, cultural heritage, and visual quality) that benefit the nearby community and society as a whole.

Agriculture Offers Many Benefits

Historical examples of agriculture from around the world would suggest that as a land use, agriculture is inherently multifunctional, offering a number of public benefits beyond the provision of commodity outputs. However, the industrialization of agriculture, particularly in the U.S. and other developed countries, has resulted in landscapes that are strongly production-oriented, often neglecting the cultural and ecological functions that had previously been supported by agricultural activities. As a result, Americans often overlook the enormous benefits that agriculture could provide, if these systems were designed for multifunctionality. A transition of agriculture to strong multifunctionality should be the desired outcome with the greatest benefits for society. Urban and peri-urban farms offer unique potential for strong multifunctionality, and their location near dense population centers could improve the successful transfer of benefits from these agricultural activities. The real challenge is to design our urban landscapes for a wide range of functions, based on the specific context of the site, while exploring synergies and focusing on positive externalities that benefit the urban society. In addition, the intentional establishment of physical linkages and cultural connections between urban agriculture and rural agriculture could provide positive outcomes beyond the limits of the city.

Local Production Is Better

The most obvious benefits of urban agriculture are related to the production of foods in close proximity to the consumers. The

Multifunctional Land Use

The Municipality of Beijing (China) is promoting the development of peri-urban agro-tourism both in the form of larger agro-recreational parks as well as family-based agro-tourism: farmers diversifying their activities by offering services to urban tourists (food, accommodation, sales of fresh and processed products, functioning as tourist guide, horse riding, etc.). The local government made agro-tourism part of municipal and district level planning; established an agro-tourism association and information dissemination service; assists interested farmers with business planning, tax exemptions and funding of infrastructure development, and provides subsidised water and electricity.

*H. de Zeeuw, M. Dubbeling, R. van Veen-
huizen, and J. Wilbers, "Courses of Action
for Municipal Policy Making on Urban Agriculture," Organic Consumers Association, 2007.*

availability of fresh fruits, vegetables, and other foods for urban residents should not be underestimated, particularly in communities and neighborhoods where grocery stores and markets have moved out, leaving a "food desert." In some cases, the food is consumed directly by the producer, improving the food security (access to healthy and culturally acceptable food) for the household. In other cases, much of the food is sold through local markets, providing income for individual residents and economic vitality for the community. Urban agriculture activities are broad and diverse and can include the cultivation of vegetables, medicinal plants, spices, mushrooms, fruit trees, and other productive plants, as well as the keeping of livestock for eggs, milk, meat, wool, or other products. By using intensive production strategies and focusing on high value crops, the economic value of urban agriculture systems can be substantial. An urban farm in Milwaukee, Wisconsin, for example, grosses more than $200,000 per acre (0.405 hectares).

For the greater public, the ecological functions and environmental benefits of urban agriculture often outweigh the production functions. By producing food locally and balancing production with consumption, the embodied energy of the food required to feed the cities is reduced because of lower transportation distance, less packaging and processing, and greater efficiency in the production inputs. The reduced energy requirements could in turn decrease greenhouse gas emissions and global warming impacts compared with conventional food systems. Energy is also conserved by reusing urban waste products locally, both biodegradable wastes for compost, and wastewater (e.g., stormwater and greywater) for irrigation. The reuse of wastes offers another benefit in reducing transportation and land use requirements for disposal and long-term management, essentially closing the loop in the cycle of waste resources. Urban agriculture, like urban gardens, can also contribute to biodiversity conservation, particularly when native species are integrated into the system. These systems can offer additional ecological benefits in modifying the urban micro-climate by regulating humidity, reducing wind, and providing shade.

Greening the City

Compared with rural agriculture, the integration of urban agriculture into densely populated areas greatly extends the opportunities for combining food production with cultural functions on urban green space. In situations where food production occurs on vacant lots or other derelict land, the effect of greening the neighborhood alone is a positive outcome for all residents in terms of visual quality and human health and well-being. The entire community also benefits from the creation of new jobs for residents who struggle to find work, from opportunities to socialize and cooperate with friends and family, and from the environmental awareness that comes from a connection to an agroecological system. By improving access to fresh, nutritious food, urban agriculture can help in combating childhood obesity, diabetes, and poor nutrition that are prevalent in many urban communities. Residents participating in community gardens and school gardens have healthier diets, consuming more fruits and vegetables than non-participants. Urban agriculture can also be very effective in providing a community with access to rare foods that support their cultural heritage, particularly for immigrant communities. Studies have demonstrated additional social benefits of community gardens through their role in improving interracial relationships and decreasing crime. Beyond the benefits for the community, individuals participating directly in the production of food enjoy the recreation and relaxation of gardening outdoors. They feel more empowered as they improve the food security of the household and gain new knowledge and technical skills. In fact, in school gardens and other community programs, the educational component can extend beyond production to include knowledge development in cooking, nutrition, science, environment, business management, and cultural sensitivity or understanding.

Farming Left Out of Urban Planning

Despite the enormous benefits for individuals and communities, urban agriculture is largely ignored in urban and regional planning. Instead of considering opportunities to preserve farmland or to integrate new production functions into urban environments, agricultural landscapes are often considered by land use planners as areas for future development. Because planners and policymakers are not typically engaged in the production activities of agriculture, they often overlook problems and opportunities within the entire food system. As a result, we see a growing disconnect between urban residents and the agricultural landscapes that sustain them. Further exacerbating the problem is the globalized economy, which encourages the importation of food from distance sources. While this approach has not threatened the availability of food for most communities in the United States (at least in terms of quantity), the increased consolidation of food systems activities, along with the concentration of agricultural land ownership, takes control away from local communities and threatens food security in the future. A community dependent on food resources from distant locations is vulnerable to any unforeseen disasters (natural or otherwise) or disruptions at different levels of the food systems chain from production through processing and transport to distribution centers.

By neglecting activities related to food systems, planners are missing a great opportunity to use something as essential and enjoyable as food, in their efforts to develop healthy communities that support a good quality of life. Food, as one of the basic essentials of life, has been almost completely avoided as an organizing strategy for improving communities. For example, rarely are urban agriculture features such as community gardens given the same level of importance as other open green space, and the result has been a lack of inclusion in the city planning process or zoning to protect them. Urban areas often require the greatest effort, but also offer the greatest potential reward in the integration of local food systems in planning, primarily because of the high densities of consumers and large proportion of poor living in cities. Planners, because of their large-scale perspective, could play an important role in designing urban areas to include community gardens and other urban agriculture features, protecting these features through appropriate zoning, and even regulating the number (or area) required per capita. Urban planners could also consider farmers markets', farm-to-institution programs, and local food networks to connect growers with processors, restaurants, groceries, and direct to consumer purchasing. Transportation systems to distribute food and waste, considering accessibility by residents, are also an urban planning opportunity. In many ways, urban planners are uniquely positioned to coordinate activities across fields, allowing urban agriculture to live up to its full potential as a multifunctional and sustainable land use.

| "Creating a sustainable food supply system now will strengthen our national security."

Urban Agriculture Will Increase National Security

Kathryn A. Peters

Kathryn A. Peters is a student in the Graduate Program in Agricultural and Food Law at the University of Arkansas School of Law. In the following viewpoint, Peters argues that developing a large-scale urban agriculture system in the United States will protect citizens from a natural or human-made disaster, thereby increasing national security, and allow the country to avoid inevitable food scarcity problems that will, she believes, inevitably affect US food imports. In addition she asserts a safe, reliable, locally based food delivery system will protect the country from food-based bioterrorism threats. According to Peters, eliminating dependence on foreign sources of energy is directly related to the US food system because so much food is imported into the country from abroad. Regarding national security, reliable availability of locally sourced food would render threats on transportation systems less severe and would also lessen the effects of an energy shortage or exorbitantly high gas prices. Urban-based agriculture run according to sustainable, organic methods, Peters concludes, would

Kathryn A. Peters, "Creating a Sustainable Urban Agriculture Revolution," *Journal of Environmental Law and Litigation*, vol. 25, no. 1, Spring 2010, pp. 204–206, 228–230. Copyright © 2010. All rights reserved. Reproduced by permission.

reduce dependence on foreign energy sources by avoiding the use of chemical-based pesticides and herbicides and eliminate the need to transport food thousands of miles to reach its market.

As you read, consider the following questions:

1. What two things does Peters say are vital to our current food supply system?
2. What is it about industrial agriculture that increases the risk of bioterrorism, according to the author?
3. According to Peters, under what conditions would the cost of transporting food become too expensive?

An adequate food supply is essential for the survival of the human race. Historically, the U.S. food system has been one of abundance. However, degradation of the environment, climate change, dependence on foreign oil and food imports, urban development trends, and increased demand due to population growth and the emerging biofuel industry all threaten our food supply. In response to these threats, local-food and sustainable agriculture movements have recently formed to raise awareness of the need to pursue alternatives to the current system. In 2009, the White House acknowledged the importance of changing the way we grow food by planting an organic garden on its grounds. In the wake of the economic crisis of 2008, victory gardens, which were first made popular during the World War II era, have reemerged and created additional awareness of the need to pursue food production alternatives. Victory gardens and local, sustainable agriculture reduce dependency on the established food production system, but, because the U.S. population is clustered in densely populated metropolitan areas, the majority of the population currently lacks access to land on which to grow food.

In the face of environmental, economic, and social equity challenges, it is imperative that the government, at federal, state, and local levels, establish policies that promote sustainable urban agriculture to ensure access to an adequate food supply produced with minimal impact on the environment. Environmental threats stemming from climate change and the depletion and degradation of natural resources will increasingly impact the planet's food production system. The current economic crisis has increased the burden on the government to provide relief in the forms of unemployment compensation and supplemental nutrition assistance. An inherent consequence of the economic crisis is a widening disparity between the rich and poor and increased social inequity between the socioeconomic classes in America. Establishing a sustainable urban agricultural system would reduce the environmental degradation that is caused by modern agricultural practices, reduce the financial strain on government resources by increasing urban productivity and enabling urbanites to grow a local food supply, and reduce socioeconomic disparities by providing less-advantaged populations in urban areas with access to an adequate supply of fresh, nutritious food. . . .

National Security

In order to be capable of sustaining itself, the United States must eliminate dependence on foreign oil and food imports. Dependence on foreign oil and food imports makes the United States vulnerable to an attack on the existing import-reliant system. Further, in order to protect U.S. interests in foreign oil, the United States funds wars and military troops overseas while many U.S. residents struggle to survive. These funds could be employed to bolster the U.S. economy and provide additional education, healthcare, housing, and food to U.S. residents, all of which would promote social equity. As the vast majority of Americans reside in urban areas, adequate energy supply and transportation infrastructure are vital to our current food supply system. A sustainable society capable of providing basic necessities within each community would sharply reduce the impact of an attack on the existing infrastructure or an energy supply shortage.

Imported Fuel Dependency

An industrial agricultural system is inherently dependent on fuel and energy for food production, transportation, and storage. Distribution of food in such a system is not only dependent on oil, but also transportation infrastructure. An attack on the oil supply or the transportation infrastructure would have an immediate and drastic impact on the food supply. Industrial mono-cultural farming in the United States, focused on large-scale production of only the most profitable crops, threatens national security by creating dependency on foreign imports to supplement the domestic food supply. Yet another threat to food security stems from the risk of bioterrorism; centralized food production sites and complex food distribution systems increase the opportunity for bioterrorist attacks on the food supply. Eventual food scarcity resulting from declining crop yields through industrial agricultural methods may lead to resource wars, further jeopardizing national security.

Urban development, like industrial agriculture, is reliant upon oil and energy to function. Declining oil and energy supplies will lead to escalating financial costs for commuting. In the face of an oil shortage, current development trends may cease to be viable as commuting via oil-dependent automobile transportation will become prohibitively expensive or, if oil is no longer available, even impossible. Similarly, the cost of transporting goods such as food will become increasingly expensive.

Urban Gardens Promote Security

Urban gardens promote both national security and food security. A local sustainable agricultural system is not dependent upon foreign oil to produce chemical fertilizers, run farm equipment, or transport food to market. Under this type of a system, threats to the food supply, in the form of oil shortages or oil price increases, would be diminished. Demand for food imports also decreases as local communities provide themselves with a constant supply of fresh food. Establishing local food production and distribution networks would reduce food scarcity vulnerabilities in the event of an attack on U.S. transportation infrastructures.

As the world population continues to grow, food scarcity will become a reality. While the United States currently relies on food imports to supplement domestic production, worldwide food scarcity will undoubtedly impact food supplies available for importation. Urban agriculture fosters national security by reducing the risk of bioterrorism and other attacks on the food supply. Creating a sustainable food supply system now will strengthen our national security and ensure that an adequate supply of fresh and healthy food is available to all U.S. residents.

Periodical and Internet Sources Bibliography

The following articles have been selected to supplement the diverse views presented in this chapter.

Jennifer Alsever	"Urban Farming 2.0: No Soil, No Sun," CNNMoney, December 23, 2010. www.cnnmoney.com.
Anne C. Bellows and Joe Nasr, eds.	"On the Past and the Future of the Urban Agriculture Movement: Reflections in Tribute to Jac Smit," special section, *Journal of Agriculture, Food Systems, and Community Development*, December 2010.
T.A. Frail	"The Rise of Urban Farming," *Smithsonian Magazine*, August 2010.
Duncan Graham-Rowe	"Are Vertical Farms the Future of Urban Food?," *Guardian* (Manchester, UK), July 29, 2010.
Julian Jackson	"Urban Agriculture—the Way of the Future?," *Earth Times*, April 26, 2011.
Jonathan Lerner	"Eat Your Subdivision," *Landscape Architect Magazine*, February 8, 2011.
Daniel Nairn	"The Future of Urban Agriculture Is Not About the 10-Mile Diet," *Grist*, October 19, 2010.
Tom Philpott	"The History of Urban Agriculture Should Inspire Its Future," *Grist*, August 3, 2010.
Karl Sharro	"Grow Your Own? Urban Farming: The Future of Food or Arcadia on the Cheap?," *Culture Wars*, September 3, 2010.

For Further Discussion

Chapter 1

1. Alison Blay-Palmer and Andy Fisher both discuss the Cuban system of mostly organic urban farming. While they agree that the system has worked for Cuba, Blay-Palmer believes the Cuban experience has broader applications in Western countries. Considering the living conditions in many of America's poorest urban communities, do you think any of the principles or techniques used in Cuba's organic urban farming can be applied to those farming in those communities? Do you think the farming and food cooperatives run by Will Allen that Roger Bybee discusses compare with the system in Cuba? Explain.

2. Nina Haletky and Owen Taylor suggest that food insecurity could be effectively fought by designing cities that include spaces for farming. But urban people who experience food insecurity already live in existing cities that were designed and built decades and even centuries ago. Can you think of design ideas that would address food insecurity for those cities? What can existing cities do to update the ways they were designed for the realities of twenty-first-century problems?

Chapter 2

1. The viewpoint by Paule Moustier and George Danso addresses the economics of urban farming in developing countries, and the one by the group Green for All discusses urban farming in terms of start-up costs and potential for profit in US cities. What do you imagine the differences and similarities to be between people who choose to farm in cities in developing countries and those who farm in American cities?

2. Isaiah Thompson argues that Philadelphia's urban farms need the support and encouragement of city government if they are to succeed financially and bring economic development to the city. Why do you think city governments might hesitate to embrace urban agriculture as a form of economic development?

3. Sena Christian argues that the urban agriculture movement has so far had a hard time demonstrating that farming in the city can be a profitable enterprise and that most urban farms continue to depend on financial support from grants and foundations in order to operate. Do you think profitability matters? Are there other ways in which cities can benefit economically from the presence of urban farms, even if they are run as nonprofits? Explain.

4. John Gallagher notes that many Detroiters are skeptical of businessman John Hantz's plan to bring large-scale commercial agriculture to Detroit. Do you think their concerns are valid? Why or why not?

Chapter 3

1. Taking into consideration Krishna Ramanujan's discussion of African Americans' response to urban farming, why do you think reactions to farming vary so much by age? What historical and social factors might account for it? Contrast this with the factors that have led Latinos to embrace urban farming, as discussed by Brenda Becerra.

2. In Max Haiven's interview with Silvia Federici, Federici says that urban agriculture is becoming "politicized." What do you think this means and how do you think it relates to the way the Detroit Black Community Food Security Network and Latino immigrants are approaching urban farming? Or do you agree with Federici's argument? Explain your answer.

3. Richard Longworth maintains that urban farming serves a "niche" market of higher-income earners rather than low-

income urbanites and suggests that what low-income city residents really need are so-called big-box discount stores like Wal-Mart. Given the argument that most cities do, in fact, have smaller, independently owned, food markets within reasonable distance of residents, do you think the presence of stores like Wal-Mart would help or hurt local economies? Could locally owned stores compete with Wal-Mart in terms of price and selection? Or would smaller markets owned by neighborhood residents be forced out of business?

Chapter 4

1. Shanon C. Kearney cites four different kinds of "capital"—economic, social, environmental, and human—and argues that city planners must take all four into consideration when planning communities. Do you think city planners of the past considered these factors when they designed older cities? Why or why not? If so, do you think those elements were forgotten or abandoned over time? If not, what are the things around which cities were organized in the past?

2. Domenic Vitiello and Michael Nairn maintain that urban agriculture is thriving even without the support of city governments and largely outside of the dominant market economy. Going back to Max Haiven's interview with Silvia Federici, do you think that urban farming in general can be considered a political movement? If so, what do you think its message might be?

3. Kathryn A. Peters argues that urban farms offer essential protection from natural and human-made disasters as well as protection from rising fuel prices. How do you think these larger issues relate to the benefits of urban agriculture discussed in other viewpoints? Consider, for example, the issues of family budgets and increased social interaction emphasized in the viewpoint by Brenda Becerra as well as the issue of food security discussed in Chapter 1.

Organizations to Contact

The editors have compiled the following list of organizations concerned with the issues debated in this book. The descriptions are derived from materials provided by the organizations. All have publications or information available for interested readers. The list was compiled on the date of publication of the present volume; names; addresses, phone and fax numbers, and e-mail and Internet addresses may change. Be aware that many organizations take several weeks or longer to respond to inquiries, so allow as much time as possible.

Alternative Farming Systems Information Center (AFSIC)
National Agricultural Library
10301 Baltimore Ave., Room 132
Beltsville, MD 20705
(301) 504-6559 • fax: (301) 504-6409
e-mail: afsic@nal.usda.gov
website: http://afsic.nal.usda.gov

A branch of the United States Department of Agriculture, the AFSIC is focused on farming-related topics that center on sustainability and alternative agricultural systems, including organic farming, aquaculture, Community Supported Agriculture, and urban farming.

American Community Gardening Association (ACGA)
1777 E. Broad Street
Columbus, OH 43203
toll-free: (877) ASK-ACGA • fax: (614) 645-5921
e-mail: info@communitygarden.org
website: http://communitygarden.org

The ACGA was founded in 1979 as a resource for community gardeners to connect with others, share information, and increase awareness of community gardening as an environmentally sustainable way to grow food. The group holds training events and workshops, publishes informational materials, and hosts an annual conference.

American Farmland Trust
1200 Eighteenth Street NW, Suite 800
Washington, DC 20036
(202) 331-7300 • fax: (202) 659-8339
e-mail: info@farmland.org
website: www.farmland.org

The American Farmland Trust opposes the development of American farm and ranch land and supports small and family farming as well as local growers across the United States. Founded in 1980, American Farmland Trust publishes research and studies on the state of American farmers, ranchers, and sustainable growing practices.

Center for Urban Agriculture at Fairview Gardens
598 N. Fairview Ave.
Goleta, CA 93117
(805) 967-7369 • fax: (805) 967-0188
e-mail: fairviewg@aol.com website:
www.fairviewgardens.org

Fairview Gardens is believed to be California's oldest organic farm, dating to 1895, and its Center for Urban Agriculture was established in 1997 to help preserve and operate the farm, as well as to provide educational and cultural opportunities to the growing suburban community surrounding the farm.

Community Food Security Coalition (CFSC)
3830 SE Division Street
Portland, OR 97202
(503) 954-2970 • fax: (503) 954-2970
e-mail: andy@foodsecurity.org
website: www.foodsecurity.org

CFSC brings together three hundred North American organizations whose concerns include hunger, poverty, sustainability, community development, economic justice, and alternative agriculture, among others, to advocate for local, state, and federal policy changes, provide training and technical assistance for community projects, and provide networking and educational resources.

Detroit Black Community Food Security Network (DBCFSN)

3800 Puritan Street
Detroit, MI 48238
(313) 345-3663
website: http://detroitblackfoodsecurity.org

DBCFSN is a nonprofit organization focusing on increasing food justice in Detroit's black community. It seeks to influence public food and agricultural policy, promote urban agriculture, encourage healthy eating habits among lower-income residents, and provide training and education to urban young people in the areas of agriculture and other food-related fields.

Food and Agriculture Organisation of the United Nations (FAO)

Viale delle Terme di Caracalla
Rome, Italy 00153
+39 06 57051 • fax: +39 06 570 53152
e-mail: fao-hq@fao.org
website: www.fao.org

The FAO focuses on eliminating hunger through rural and urban development programs that address subjects including aquaculture, gender equality, natural resources, and emergency food distribution. The FAO publishes annual reports and subject papers related to its programs.

International Development Research Centre (IDRC)
150 Kent St.
Ottawa, ON, Canada K1P 0B2
(613) 236-6163 • fax: (613) 238-7230
e-mail: info@idrc.ca
website: www.idrc.ca

The IDRC promotes economic growth and social justice in developing countries through research, fellowships, and funding for various projects. The IRDC publishes annual reports and funds researchers in poor countries, including those working in the agricultural field.

Just Food
1155 Avenue of the Americas, 3rd floor
New York, NY 10036
(212) 645-9880, ext. 221
e-mail: info@justfood.org
website: www.justfood.org

Just Food works to bring locally grown food to New York City neighborhoods, particularly those that lack adequate access to healthy, fresh foods, by promoting Community Supported Agriculture (CSA) projects, city farms, food cooperatives, and food justice initiatives.

Resource Centres on Urban Agriculture and Food Security Foundation (RUAF Foundation)
PO Box 64, 3830
AB Leusden, The Netherlands
+31 33 4326039 • fax: +31 33 4940791
e-mail: ruaf@etcnl.nl
website: www.ruaf.org

The RUAF Foundation is an international partnership of one global and seven regional research centers. The primary goals of the foundation are to study the use of urban agriculture for economic development, poverty alleviation, and food insecurity, as well as to study and encourage the participation of women in urban agriculture.

University of Georgia Center for Urban Agriculture

1109 Experiment Street
Griffin, GA 30223-1797
(770) 233-6107
website: http://apps.caes.uga.edu/urbanag

The University of Georgia's Center for Urban Agriculture is a research, teaching, and extension resource that combines a focus on developing sustainable urban agriculture with an interest in urban economic development. The center publishes papers and engages members of the university, industry, and the public to provide an interdisciplinary approach.

Urban Farming

19785 W. 12 Mile Road #537
Southfield, MI 48076
(313) 664-0615; toll-free: (877) 679-8300
e-mail: info@urbanfarming.org
website: www.urbanfarming.org

Urban Farming is a Detroit area–based organization that has established "empowerment zones" throughout the United States in which it helps communities develop urban gardens. The group hosts education and job training classes, business and urban development seminars, and health and wellness forums in addition to promoting urban farming as a way to address food insecurity and injustice.

Bibliography of Books

Novella Carpenter

Farm City: The Education of an Urban Farmer. New York: Penguin, 2010.

Dickson Despommier

The Vertical Farm: Feeding the World in the 21st Century. New York: Thomas Dunne Books, 2010.

Nigel Dunnett and Noël Kingsbury

Planting Green Roofs and Living Walls. Portland, OR: Timber Press, 2008.

Heather C. Flores

Food Not Lawns: How to Turn Your Yard into a Garden and Your Neighborhood into a Community. White River Junction, VT: Chelsea Green, 2006.

Mark Gorgolewski, June Komisar, and Joe Nasr

Carrot City: Creating Places for Urban Agriculture. New York: Monacelli Press, 2011.

Robert Gottlieb and Anupama Joshi

Food Justice. Cambridge, MA: MIT Press, 2010.

Jeffrey Hou, Julie M. Johnson, and Laura J. Lawson

Greening Cities, Growing Communities: Learning from Seattle's Urban Community Gardens. Seattle: University of Washington Press, 2009.

Scott Kellogg

Toolbox for Sustainable City Living: A Do-It-Ourselves Guide. Cambridge, MA: South End Press, 2008.

Barbara Kilarski   *Keep Chickens! Tending Small Flocks in Cities, Suburbs, and Other Small Spaces.* North Adams, MA: Storey, 2003.

Patricia Klindienst   *The Earth Knows My Name: Food, Culture, and Sustainability in the Gardens of Ethnic America.* Boston: Beacon, 2006.

Mustafa Koc, Rod MacRae, Jennifer Welsh, and Luc J.A. Mugeot, eds.   *For Hunger-Proof Cities: Sustainable Urban Food Systems.* Ottawa, ON: IDRC Books, 2000.

Janine de La Salle and Mark Holland, eds.   *Agricultural Urbanism: Handbook for Building Sustainable Food Systems in 21st-Century Cities.* Winnipeg, MB Green Frigate Books, 2010.

Laura J. Lawson   *City Bountiful: A Century of Community Gardening in America.* Berkeley: University of California Press, 2005.

Thomas A. Lyson   *Civic Agriculture: Reconnecting Farm, Food, and Community.* Boston: Tufts Univ. Press, 2004.

Ian Marvy   "Youth Empowerment Through Urban Agriculture: Red Hook Community Farm," in *Restorative Commons: Creating Health and Well-Being Through Urban Landscapes*, edited by Lindsay Campbell and Anne Wiesen.

General Technical Report
NRS-P-39, U.S. Department
of Agriculture, Forest Service,
Northern Research Station, 2009.

Luc J.A. Mugeot, ed.   *Agropolis: The Social, Political,*
and Environmental Dimensions
of Urban Agriculture. Oxford,UK:
Earthscan, 2005.

Luc J.A. Mugeot, ed.   *Growing Better Cities: Urban*
Agriculture for Sustainable
Development. Ottawa, ON: IDRC
Books, 2006.

Darrin Nordahl   *Public Produce: The New Urban*
Agriculture. Washington, DC:
Island, 2009.

Michael Perry   *Coop: A Year of Poultry, Pigs,*
and Parenting. New York:
HarperCollins, 2009.

Michael Pollan   *The Omnivore's Dilemma.* New
York: Penguin, 2007.

Jeremy N. Smith   *Growing a Garden City:*
How Farmers, First Graders,
Counselors, Troubled Teens,
Foodies, a Homeless Shelter Chef,
Single Mothers and More Are
Transforming Themselves and
Their Neighborhoods Through the
Intersection of Local Agriculture
and Community—and You Can
Too. New York: Skyhorse, 2010.

Lisa Taylor | *Your Farm in the City: An Urban-Dweller's Guide to Growing Food and Raising Animals.* New York: Black Dog & Leventhal, 2011.

David Tracey | *Urban Agriculture: Ideas and Designs for the New Food Revolution.* Gabriola Island, BC: New Society, 2011.

Andre Viljoen | *Continuous Productive Urban Landscapes: Designing Agriculture for Sustainable Cities.* Amsterdam: Architectural Press, 2005.

Mark Winne | *Closing the Food Gap: Resetting the Table in the Land of Plenty.* Boston: Beacon, 2009.

Mark Winne | *Food Rebels, Guerilla Gardeners, and Smart-Cookin' Mamas: Fighting Back in an Age of Industrial Agriculture.* Boston: Beacon, 2006.

Index